CREATE WEALTH
WITH HOMEOWNERSHIP

LESSONS ON BUYING AND OWNING A HOME & IMPROVING NET WORTH

DOUGLAS BONCOSKY

DNA Press™

©2009 DNA Press, LLC

CREATE WEALTH WITH HOMEOWNERSHIP:
LESSONS ON BUYING AND OWNING A HOME & IMPROVING NET WORTH
©Copyright by Douglas Boncosky
©2009 DNA Press, LLC. All rights reserved.

Library of Congress Cataloging-in-Publication Data

Boncosky, Douglas. Create Wealth With Homeownership : Lessons on Buying and Owning a Home & Improving Net Worth / Douglas Boncosky. — 1st ed.
     p. cm.

ISBN 978-1-933255-48-4

     (pbk. : alk. paper)

1. House buying—United States. 2. Mortgage loans—United States. I. Title.
     HD259.B64 2009
     333.33'80973—dc22

     2 0 0 9 0 1 8 9 9 4

DNA Press, LLC
www.dnapress.com
editors@dnapress.com

Publisher: DNA Press, LLC
Executive Editor: Alexander Kuklin, Ph.D.
Copy Editor: Sunila Samuel
Art Direction: Alex Nartea
Cover Art & Graphics: Gina Hutchings

Acknowledgements

I want to thank my wife Debby for her love, support, and patience. Without her, I would not have been able to dedicate the time necessary to write this book. She provided insights that helped tremendously in the creation of this book, and I'm lucky to have her in my life.

I want to thank my editor, Sunila Samuel. If it weren't for her friendship with my wife, I would have not found such a great editor to help me shape this book. I thank her not only for her insight and perspective, but also for the long hours and late nights she put in to have this book finished on time.

I want to thank Gina Hutchings of Lunarmedia.net for the cover layout and interior artwork. She is a creative genius in both print and web design and a dedicated professional with whom I have had the pleasure to work on various projects for quite a few years.

I wish I knew then what I know now.

(*author unknown*)

Hindsight is 20/20, and nowhere is that more radically evident than in personal financial management. When I look back at the financial decisions I made in my late 20s, I realize that some of them may not have been the most prudent because of my lack of knowledge. The same can be said for most people with whom I have met to discuss their mortgage. Yet, I learned from the missteps I made and I used that knowledge to make wiser decisions thereafter. My wish is that after reading this book, you learn to avoid the missteps that I and so many others have made and you subsequently apply these lessons to your own life and, 10 to 20 years from now, you are as financially better off.

TABLE OF CONTENTS

FOREWORD

If you have done some traveling by plane during the course of life, I'm sure that you have been entertained by the people in the airport like I have been. And, if you have ever arrived at your gate and scanned the sea of people waiting to board your flight or board flights at nearby gates, you may have noticed that, at least for me, they fall into two categories: those who have already purchased their ticket and those who are flying standby. I can always spot those passengers who already have their ticket and their confirmed seat assignment because they are the ones who are peacefully waiting and very relaxed as they read a magazine or book, check email on their laptop, or take a quick snooze before boarding.

Those flying standby, on the other hand, are hovered around the counter at the gate, nervously pacing the boarding area and anxiously awaiting news of their fate—will they or will they not have a seat on this flight? I'm sure that you know exactly who I am talking about. You may have even been one of them. And as we watch our fellow travelers linger in this abyss of uncertainty, you almost feel bad for them, but at the same time, you have to admit that they allowed themselves to be in such a situation.

You can liken this situation to living a financially healthy life, which is the main message of this book. Buying a home, saving for the unexpected, and preparing for retirement can have a significant impact on your financial life. There are those in life who prepare ahead of time, purchase their ticket, and reserve their seat on a flight to financial security and stability. However, there are others who take their chances, don't necessarily plan, and find themselves sometimes left behind watching their flight to financial health depart without them.

Either way, some turbulence such as job loss, medical expenses, changing economy, will most certainly be part of this journey; however, how you prepare yourself financially, using specific tools, will allow you to handle any turbulence along the way. Those who don't save or manage their finances properly or buy too much home will likely remain on standby, perhaps watching with regret as others—those who are boarding the plane to financial security—enjoy a more comfortable life and retirement.

I have sat down with many people in their mid- to late-60s who have contacted me to help them, for example, with a debt consolidation loan because they had up to this point lived their lives flying standby, watching plane after plane take off without them. I have also helped many people take advantage of lower interest rates and step up to larger homes to support their growing family; they were able to accomplish this only because they were prepared by having properly managed their finances for such a change.

While there are plenty of people in our world today who appear to have done everything perfectly, things aren't always what they seem to be. For example, your neighbors in the house next door could appear as if they have it together as they are always well dressed, drive nice new cars, have all the upgrades in their home, and take nice trips. The husband went off to work everyday while the wife worked at home taking care of the kids and maintaining the house. From the outside looking in, everything seemed to be perfect. But, in reality they were flying standby even though you would have bet that they had secured seats on the flight. If you really knew the reality of their situation, you would know that they were not prepared. They were living paycheck to paycheck. All the nice clothes and trips were paid for by credit cards, they had $75,000 in credit card debt, the cars were leased, and very little cash to save for retirement. They stopped contributing to their retirement accounts through work and started taking withdrawals from those accounts to maintain their supposedly perfect lifestyle. One medical emergency that insurance does not cover or a job loss, and this family will find themselves losing their home. By no means were they on the flight to a comfortable retirement, they were a ball of nerves flying standby trying to maintain a perception. They were living a financial lie.

My point in giving you this analogy is to emphasize how important homeownership can be to your financial well being. We can all live the American Dream of owning a home, but I want to show you how to do it by making wise choices. I hope to teach you how to decide on how much home to buy while taking advantage of the benefits that homeownership can provide. At the same time, saving and investing for retirement cannot be overlooked, but must play an integral part of your overall plan. Striking a balance between owning a home, saving, and investing will give you the peace of mind that your flight will reach its destination. So you decide: which type of passenger do you want to be on the flight to financial security?

INTRODUCTION

From my analogy in the forward you can gather that Create Wealth with Homeownership was written to help you understand the right way to buy a home with the sole purpose of letting that home work for you over time in combination with your savings and retirement goals to reach a healthy retirement. With such life changing and important concepts, I wish I had four to five hours to sit down with each and every client I meet with to discuss these concepts in detail. Because we lead such busy lives with work, family, and leisure time activities, I have yet to meet with a client who has that much time to sit down for a long chat. And as much as I would like to, I do not have the time either to spend with each client in one sitting. Besides, after meeting in person for an extended period, clients' eyes begin to glaze over from the information overload.

Over the years, I have had so many questions from and "a-ha" moments with clients that I decided to write this book to share my message. With this book, clients and future homeowners across America can learn these important concepts on their own time. For those who have already gone through the homebuying process, there are chapters worth reading, as you might not have been aware of some of these concepts when you bought your home.

To help you understand how to create wealth with homeownership, I have organized the book into three parts.

Part 1 - Why Own The Home You Live In
Developing an understanding about the financial reasons for own-ing a home is the integral to improving your net worth. Without them, you will have no basis on which to grow the financial side of your life. Here you will learn about appreciation and why it ex-ists, why the net worth of homeowners is 12 times greater than that of renters, the power of compound interest when saving and in-vesting, and why owning a home and saving/investing at the same time will generate a healthy net worth over time.

Part 2 - The Homebuying Process

Once you develop a financial understanding of why you want to own a home, you can then move into learning about the sometimes overwhelming homebuying process. Here you will learn about figuring out how much home you can afford, understanding credit, getting pre-approved, shopping for a home, and reaching the big closing day when you pick up the keys to your new home.

Part 3 - Life as a Homeowner

After you buy a home, you will need to not only protect your investment, but also help grow its value and your net worth. In this part you will learn about maintaining and improving your home, protecting your investment using various types of insurance coverage, and reducing your cost of money with lower interest rates by refinancing. These are steps that will either save you thousands in interest costs by paying off your mortgage early or help you create thousands in interest earnings by keeping your mortgage long-term.

If you are a first-time homebuyer, then reading the entire book will be helpful. More than likely, once you purchase a home, you will come back to Part 3 to review some concepts. If you already own a home or are considering moving to a new home, then reading Parts 1 and 3 will be very helpful.

As you know, the title of this book is Create Wealth with Homeownership, Not "Get Rich with Homeownership." Wealth is defined differently for different people. However, my definition of wealth in this book is the point in time when your assets exceed your debts, also commonly known as your freedom point. The sooner you reach your freedom point, the sooner you will create wealth for you and your family to live a more comfortable life. When your assets exceed your debts, you have the freedom to do some things that you would not ordinarily be able to do if you had to continue to pay your mortgage or other debts for your entire life.

By no means is this book designed to help you "get rich quick" by owning a home. This is practical information that, when used the right way, will help you to live a comfortable life within your means while providing a roof over your and/or your family's heads, all while the home you're living in is appreciating in value over time.

Believe it or not, the way you view your home and the mortgage that goes along with it makes a huge difference in how you transition into retirement. The decisions you make today are very important and will affect your future 20, 30, and even 40 years from now.

This book starts with the fundamentals, of which you need to have a grasp before you move forward with the purchase of a home. Many people just buy a home without having knowledge of these fundamentals and figure they will learn as they go along. Thinking and learning as you go along may work when you are compulsively buying a $15 gadget that caught your eye in a store; the loss from such a decision would only be $15. However, when you are putting thousands of dollars of your hard-earned money down and signing your name to a mortgage loan that is in excess of $100,000, don't you think it would be a good idea to have a solid foundation of the financial concepts surrounding this huge transaction? The result of bad decision-making in this case could be financial ruin. Unfortunately, so many people view buying a home as a simple transaction, but in fact buying a home is rather complex when you begin to look at the financial impact it has on your life.

I am writing this book at a time when the economy is near its worst in our country's history. We are experiencing record home foreclosures, falling home values, huge job losses, government bailouts, and so much more. There is so much uncertainty that people are often not sure how to proceed.

Granted, the country's financial state is not at its best during this time, but if you panic and despair over every negative story in the news, you will find yourself in a downward spiral of depression. I tell my wife often that the only economy we need to focus on is our own. Yes, our retirement accounts and home value are down, but we are both employed, we don't plan to retire for another 25 years, we are able to pay our bills, we continue to save for our retirement, and we are still able to take vacations and do other fun activities. In the grand scheme of things, our own personal economy is okay. From that perspective, I can sleep at night.

If you are a first-time homebuyer, you have time on your side as well. As you will learn in this book, historically our economy bounces back from bad times. Historically, home values come back to where they were and grow beyond. The same can be said for your own personal investments. I am not a financial advisor, but I can tell you that in the past, people who lost value in their investments saw the return of those gains and more over time. My point is that if you are in for the long haul (30 to 40 years) when buying a home, history shows us you will be just fine.

Granted, home values have declined over the last couple of years, and they could decline even more. This decline has made buying a home very attractive for first-time homebuyers because of the lower values. At the same time however, people are concerned values could get lower. You can't predict the future or always buy a home at the lowest price, but upon reading this book you will gain the knowledge necessary to make wise judgments about your decision to buy.

In my case, I bought my home near the peak of values in 2006. However, to my credit, I bought it at a time that was right for my wife and me. I knew the conditions of our economy at the time I was buying and knew I was probably paying more than I should, but at the same time, not as much as others for similar model homes. Yet, I was not concerned with what was going to happen to values in the short-term because I bought a home within my means and had no plans to move any time soon. Besides, I know, based on the history of real estate appreciation, that my home's value will go up over time.

However, since our economy goes through cycles of good times and bad, you need to be financially prepared to deal with the bad times. One major reason that so many people are losing homes in our country right now is that they had little or no money in savings to help them weather the storm. In other words, they weren't financially prepared to deal with life's unexpected hardships.

By reading this book, you are taking a huge leap forward. You are spending the time to educate yourself about homeownership so that you can make it work for you financially. This book is not designed to tell you how to make money overnight by purchasing a home. There are plenty of other books and TV shows out there about flipping houses (but even that is not a sure bet unless you really know what you are doing).

As you will see in this book, the primary message I am sending is this: buy a home that is going to allow you to live comfortably while still being able to maintain an emergency fund and contribute to your savings and retirement accounts. In that sense, homebuying is really that simple. In my opinion, many who are losing their homes today bought more home than they could handle financially thus preventing their ability to fund savings and retirement. As a result, as soon as they had a setback in their finances from job loss, medical issues, or some other circumstance that caused a financial hardship, they found themselves behind in their mortgage payments simply because they did not have access to cash to continue making their mortgage payments.

After reading this book, you will become a prudent homebuyer. You will make the right decisions ensuring you are comfortable with your housing payment while still funding your savings and retirement accounts. Therefore, if you ever do have a problem down the line that causes financial difficulties, you will have the money to endure the storm and come out on top with just a couple of scratches instead of a ruined financial life.

Regardless of whatever conditions our economy is in, if you are considering buying a home—whether it's the day you buy this book or five years down the road—you can be confident that your investment will pay off over time. Again, this confidence will come from looking at the bigger picture and knowing that based on the history of real estate in the United States, your home will appreciate in value.

Reading this book along with others will help you find your comfort level in the homebuying process. It will also help you feel assured about your decision after you close on the purchase of your new home.

Let's begin!

PART I

WHY OWN THE HOME YOU LIVE IN

CHAPTER 1

Are You Ready to Own a Home?

Buying a home is one of the most exciting experiences in a person's life. It can also be one of the most nerve-racking. However, if you understand the steps and know what to expect, your worries about purchasing a home can be minimized, leaving you to enjoy the experience even more.

As a practicing mortgage professional, there is nothing more exciting to me than sitting with clients at the title company's closing table, where they have just signed the papers to take possession of their new home. The words I love to hear most when a client is smiling ear-to-ear are: "Thank you so much. You really made this process much less stressful."

Considering that buying a home is the largest financial transaction you will more than likely make in your lifetime, it is very important for you to have a complete understanding as to the financial reasons behind owning a home and the process for buying a home.

The purpose of this book is not only to ease your mind about this overwhelming and complicated process, but also to give you insight as to how this home purchase will impact your financial life now and how it will affect you in the future.

Owning a home is a big responsibility. The homebuying process can be intimidating and seem personally intrusive, especially for a first-time homebuyer. The questions you should ask and answer yourself before taking on this endeavor are:

- *Should I continue to rent?*
- *When is the right time to purchase a home?*
- *Can I afford to buy a home?*
- *Do I really want to own a home?*
- *Why do I want to own a home?*

By the time you finish reading this book, you will be equipped with the right knowledge to answer those questions as you will have developed a complete understanding of not only the financial intricacies of buying a home, but also the responsibilities that go along with homeownership.

What Is a Home?

Before I go into detail about homebuying, I want you to have a good understanding of how "home" is defined in this book. A home is a piece of residential real estate to which you hold the title. The various types of homes (which I will explain in more detail later in the book) include:

- Single-family home (a single dwelling on a piece of real estate)
- Duplex (You own the whole structure; you live in one unit and rent out the other unit.)
- 3-Flat / 4-Flat (You own the whole building; you live in one unit and rent out the others.)
- Condominium / Townhouse (You own and live in one unit that is part of a building consisting of two or more units.)

If you do not intend on actually living in any of these types of homes, then the purchase of such a home would be considered an investment property and, therefore, different qualifying guidelines would apply. The principles I talk about in this book also apply to investment properties, but I suggest reading other books pertaining to buying and managing such properties.

What Is Not Considered a Home?

In this book, there are two types of real estate that I do not consider to be a home:

- A trailer in a trailer park
- Raw land

Owning a trailer in a trailer park would not be considered owning a home because the land on which the trailer sits is owned by someone else.

The owner of the trailer is leasing/renting the space for the trailer. A loan that the owner might have for the trailer would not be considered a mortgage.

Raw land is also not considered a home. Raw land is land that you buy and on which you consider building a home at a later date. The financing available for raw land is different from the financing for a piece of residential land with an existing permanent structure on it. If you are considering building a home on a raw piece of land, then you would need a construction loan to finance the purchase of the land and the home that would be built on it. For this reason, I will not be covering construction loans in this book.

Owning Real Estate Is a Big Responsibility

Now that you're familiar with the definition of a home, let's take a look at the responsibilities that go along with owning one. Important points to consider are:

1. You are signing a huge loan secured by your new home;
2. You are using your hard-earned money for a down payment;
3. You are responsible for the repairs and upkeep of your home; and
4. You are responsible for maintaining insurance and paying your property taxes.

This list is enough to keep some people renting their entire life! However, the 68.9%[1] of America's population that own a home realize that these issues are not as significant when compared to the improved net worth that can be created from ownership.

For the remaining 31.1% who choose not to own real estate, a large portion is at the age or place in life at which owning is not yet practical. However, the sad part about many who fall into this 31.1% is that they are just too nervous or do not want to be bothered with owning, so renting the rest of their life is ok for them. As you will see in this book, not owning

---

[1] United States Census Bureau, 2005 Data, www.census.gov

the home in which you live can significantly impede you from improving your net worth.

Why Do You Want To Own a Home?

When I ask the question "Why do you want to own a home?", some of the most common answers I receive are:

- I want a place to call my own.
- We need more space for living.
- We need more space for the children.
- I want to personalize my home and yard.
- We want to be a part of a neighborhood/community.
- I want tax deductions.
- We want to build equity for retirement (wealth creation).

What do you think is most important in the list? Unfortunately, people focus on the first five items listed and pay less attention to the tax benefits or wealth creation (what I call the "financial side") of owning a home. For some people, owning is the next logical step in their life, and they decide to buy a home without really thinking about the long-term financial effects of owning. *Figure 1-1* illustrates this point with the smaller print for the financial side.

It is my belief that people don't pay much attention to the financial side of owning because they don't understand it and, therefore, shy away from it. It is in our human nature to avoid areas or subjects with which we are not familiar as we don't want to be embarrassed if we don't understand something right away. With this book, my goal is to make you comfortable with the financial side because this part of homeownership is the one that impacts your life the most—not the color of paint you choose for your walls.

When I bought my first home, which was a townhouse, I went to the local bank and gave them a bunch of papers showing my income, savings, etc. They said I could buy a home worth $150,000 or so. Looking back, I

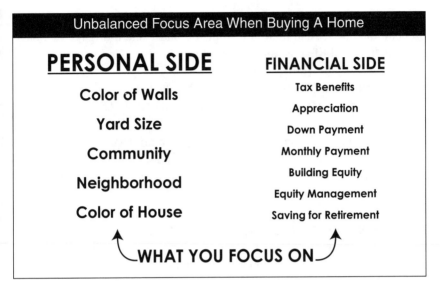

Figure 1-1

remember how nervous and excited I was, but at the same time I remember how the process was almost like opening up a checking account—just with more paperwork. No educational process came with it to help me understand what was really taking place. My knowledge was based on what I had heard in the news and learned from casual reading. I did not know about loan programs; I just took whatever loan program the bank gave me. To be honest with you, I didn't care. At that point, I just wanted to own the townhouse to have more space and to live the American Dream of owning my own place. In retrospect, I see now that I should have cared.

It was not until I became a mortgage professional that I further realized how much more important the financial side is to owning a home. As my mortgage career has evolved over time and as I have seen how people react to and deal with aspects surrounding homebuying, I have come to recognize the important details I need to share with clients to help them make wise choices regarding ownership. Because my first experience lacked any comprehensive education, the purpose of my mortgage practice is based solely on providing my clients with the right information so that they truly comprehend the impact that their new home purchase and mortgage will have on their financial life now and in the future.

Knowing what I know now, I can see that the loan program I was given by the bank at that time was not a good one. The interest rate was relative, but to purchase my home, the bank gave me a 5-year balloon loan, which local banks tend to prefer. In my practice, I would never put a client into a balloon type of loan as it exposes my client to too much risk. Later on in this book, I will share the details of balloon loans and why they are not the best option.

A Few Reasons Not to Buy a Home Now

Buying a home is not for everyone. Certain circumstances in life may prevent you from owning a home now such as:

- Lack of job security
- Knowing you will be moving within a few years
- Poor credit
- Lack of income or unverifiable income
- In the middle of a divorce

Lack of Job Security

Lenders prefer borrowers who have at least a two-year track record of employment, although I have seen people buy homes with less than a two-year job history. Considering that lending guidelines change frequently, it's best to talk with a mortgage professional about your situation if you have less than a two-year job history.

Knowing You Will Be Moving Within a Few Years

You need to be in the home you buy for at least three to four years (if not more) for it to make financial sense. Because there is a cost to buying a home, the cost of selling a home can be more expensive considering you may have to enlist the services of a real estate agent to sell the home. (You can always try to sell on your own, which will cost you some, but the vast majority of sellers enlist the services of a real estate agent.) Since the sellers pay the real estate commission, you can expect to pay 5-6% of the sale price in commission. Naturally you will have wanted the home to appreciate to cover the cost of selling; otherwise you will be taking a loss. *Figure 1-2* illustrates the costs associated with selling a home along with the appreciation you would need to break even on the sale. You will see in *Figure 1-2* that to sell this house for $180,000, you will have needed to gain $23,300 from appreciation to break even from your original purchase price after factoring in the expenses to selling a home. If current real estate appreciation levels are at 4%, it will take you roughly four years to gain $23,300 in appreciation. If appreciation levels are zero or even negative as they are at the time of this writing, you could expect to stay in your home even longer.

The one exception to potential future moves is a job transfer. Many companies who transfer employees have a relocation benefits program in

Move Up Sales Price Analysis

Analysis if selling home for $180,000

Sales Price		$180,000
6% real estate commission		$10,800
Moving expenses	+	$2,500
Improvements	+	$10,000
Total Costs	=	**$23,300**
Appreciation to break even		**$23,300**
Purchase price of home should have been		**$156,700**

Ownership time to reach appreciation of $23,300

Appreciation Rate	**3%**	**4%**	**5%**	**6%**
Years (rounded)	5 Years	4 Years	3 Years	2.5 Years

Figure 1-2

which they allocate money to you to cover the expenses of the transfer. The amount of money provided will often be more than enough to cover the real estate commission along with your moving expenses. Therefore, this commission cost may not be of concern to you. But, in such a case, you should fully understand the terms of the relocation program offered by your employer before buying if you know you have a chance of being transferred.

Poor Credit

Your credit is the most important determining factor in a lender's decision to loan you money for the purchase of a home. As you will read later on in this book, maintaining good credit is imperative to a financially rewarding life. If you have collection issues, past due accounts, or tax liens because you did not pay your taxes, your credit score is going to reflect that, and the ability to buy a home may be challenging. The Federal Housing Authority (FHA) and Veterans Administration (VA), which I will cover in the chapters ahead, have lending programs for people with less-than-perfect credit, so there is hope if your credit is not ideal.

Lack of Income or Unverifiable Income

If you have a lack of income, you either do not have a job history or you are just not being paid enough to qualify in the lender's eyes. If you earn enough, but the income is not verifiable, you are more than likely a self-employed or a commission-only professional. If this is the case, you need to work with your CPA/Tax Preparer to ensure you properly accounted for your income and expenses on your tax return. If you are not able to correct your accounting, you may have to have a co-borrower to be able to qualify for a home loan. In today's market, unlike the late 1990s and early 2000s, you need to be able to prove to a lender that you earn enough money to afford the home.

In the Middle of a Divorce

If you are in the middle of a divorce, in most cases, you will not be able to buy a home until after the divorce is settled. The reason for this is that the lender sees that there is too much risk because they do not know at this point how much you may be required to pay in alimony or child support. If the divorce decree states that you will be responsible for these costs, it will affect your income, so you may not qualify for a loan. Lenders prefer a divorce to be settled before making a decision to approve a borrower for a loan.

What You Need to Have Before Buying

Now that you know the circumstances that may prevent you from buying a home, let's summarize the essentials to purchasing a home. You need:

- Steady employment
- Average or better-than-average credit
- Money for closing costs and/or a down payment

You Need to Have Steady Employment

Typically, you will need to have an employment history of at least two years to qualify to purchase a home. Lenders prefer that your history be at the same employer, but changing from one employer to another during that time without a long gap in between will be ok. As I said earlier, there may be exceptions, so check with your mortgage professional to determine what your options may be if you have less than a two-year employment history.

You Need Average or Better-than-Average Credit

At the time of this writing, if your credit score is less than 620, it will be difficult for you to be able to purchase a home of your own. This credit score guideline does change from time to time, so you will always want to check with a mortgage professional to find out the minimum credit score needed to qualify. There was a time when a 500 credit score was the minimum. However, lenders keep raising the minimum, so I would expect to see the current minimum score of 620 to rise as time rolls along. You will learn more about credit in Chapter 6.

You Need Money for Closing Costs and/or a Down Payment

When you buy a home, there will be closing costs, and in most cases you will need down payment money. You can take advantage of grant programs, down payment assistance programs, gifts of equity, or down payment gifts to buy a home. You will learn more about this in Part 2.

Are You Ready to Buy?

In the next chapter, I will be talking about the most significant and exciting reason to own a home: the financial side.

CHAPTER 2
The Financial Impact of Homeownership

Whether this is the first or fourth home you are buying, the information contained in this chapter will change the way you think about homeownership. You will begin to make informed decisions as to how you handle the purchase of a home and the mortgage that goes along with it.

What Is a Mortgage?

Before we go any further, I must explain what exactly a mortgage is. The word mortgage is often used in place of home loan. So, when you hear people talking about their mortgage, they are really referring to their home loan. In a technical sense, a mortgage is the agreement you sign pledging your home to the lender in exchange for the home loan. I will explain more about the technical side of a mortgage in *Chapter 8*, but I wanted you to know the basic definition now since I will be talking about mortgages in this chapter.

Why Is Owning a Home Financially Beneficial?

Like me, when I bought my first home, most people buying a home are not thinking about the financial side other than figuring out how to make sure they have enough money for the down payment and closing costs. However, the sooner you begin to think a little bit more about the financial terms, the sooner you will see how significant the impact of buying a home will have on your life now, and more importantly, 10, 20, and even 30 years down the road.

To prove my point on how important homeownership is to your financial life, take a look at *Figure 2-1*. This figure illustrates the results of a study conducted by the Federal Reserve Board comparing homeowners to renters. Keep in mind the study is based on income and, therefore, does not consider how long a person has owned or rented.

As you can see, these numbers convey a pretty powerful point. The homeowner has a net worth TWELVE TIMES that of a renter in the

Net Worth of Home Owners vs. Renters		
Annual Income	**Owners**	**Renters**
$80,000 and up	$451,200	$87,400
$50,000 - $79,999	$194,610	$25,000
$30,000 - $49,999	$126,500	$10,600
$16,000 - $29,999	$112,600	$4,240
Under $16,000	$73,000	$500

Source: *Federal Reserve Board, 2004 Survey of Consumer Finance*

Figure 2-1

$30,000 to $49,999 income category. Simply speaking, all the homeowner did was change his/her housing type. Instead of paying the landlord, he/she paid a lender, and in doing so, created a greater net worth. I wish that I had this knowledge when I bought my first home at age 29!

Later in this chapter, I will show you how these differences in net worth are possible when comparing renters to owners. However, you first must have a complete understanding of real estate for that concept to make sense.

The first thing that you need to understand is equity. Equity is the difference between the value of your home and the amount you still owe on the home. For example, if your home is worth $250,000, and you owe $200,000, your equity or equity position would be $50,000. Equity is derived in three ways:

- The amount of money you put down.
- The amount of principal you pay every month to pay your mortgage balance down.
- The increase in your home's value, i.e.: appreciation.

The amount of money you put down on a home is a form of instant equity. This does not have a significant impact on creating wealth because you're just taking money you already have and putting it into your home.

The amount of principal you pay every month to pay off your loan does help you to create wealth. If you were renting, you would just continue to pay rent. By making your monthly mortgage payment, you are paying down your mortgage balance with the hopes of not having a mortgage payment some day and owning the home free and clear. This process has helped you to create equity in your home, thus increasing your net worth.

The most important reason people buy real estate is that real estate appreciates in value. This means that over time, the equity in your home will increase. In looking at *Figure 2-2*, you will see that over a five-year period, your $250,000 home would be worth $300,000 and you would have paid your loan down from $200,000 to $190,000. Your new equity position would be $110,000 rather than the $50,000 five years earlier. These are round numbers, but we will look at appreciation in more detail in a moment.

This difference between the net worth of homeowners and renters occurs for three reasons:

Understanding Equity

After five years of owning a home, equity is created by considering your original down payment, the amount you have paid down your mortgage, and the appreciation in the value of your home:

Current value of home		$300,000
Less purchase price	-	$250,000
Appreciation gained	=	**$ 50,000**
Plus paying down mortgage balance	+	$ 10,000
Plus original down payment	+	$ 50,000
Equity position after five years		**$110,000**

Figure 2-2

1. Real estate appreciates in value.
2. Tax deductions improve cash flow.
3. Homeowners have a strategy to manage mortgage debt.

Real Estate Appreciates in Value

I believe that most people understand that real estate does appreciate over time. Some, however, do not know the average appreciation for their area or that the appreciation of real estate is not consistent from one year to the next. Furthermore, real estate does not appreciate at the same rate within different parts of a city. Various economic factors affect home appreciation levels, such as the economy and the demand in your local marketplace.

For example, in the Chicago market where I am from, homes appreciated faster in the Bucktown neighborhood of Chicago than they did in the Hyde Park neighborhood. The reason for this is that there was demand for Bucktown neighborhood homes. People want to be there. New restaurants and shops were popping up along with new construction of condos and single-family homes. It is a place where people want to live, and the value of real estate reflects that, despite our current economic times.

When times are booming in our economy, the one thing you want to be careful of regarding appreciation values is focusing too much on areas that are experiencing extraordinary growth in a short period of time from new construction. One example is the town of Plainfield, Illinois. This town saw home values increase too much and too fast, and when the economy began to change in 2007, so did the real estate market. Unfortunately, residents actually saw their home values fall by $50,000 to $75,000, and they now owe more on their home than what it is worth. These people are in a tough place because if they have to sell their home now, they must be prepared for a loss. If they can stay in their home for a while, they will hopefully begin to see some of that loss reduced as real estate begins to appreciate again as our economy goes through its cycles.

This is the same reason that Arizona, California, Florida, and Nevada are seeing huge decreases in values[2]. Values were growing so fast in parts of these states that home values fell even more rapidly. In many cases, people were driving prices up so fast through speculation because of the demand for housing and the quick rise of home prices. Many investors or want-to-be investors from around the country were buying condos in Florida and then flipping them for huge profits once they were completed. This type of value increase will only go so far before it crashes. As expected, it did, and people were on the hook for losses close to $100,000 or more. This is why people just walked away from condos that were not even finished yet. When talking with your real estate agent, ask him/her to show you the appreciation history for the area in which you are looking to buy. You want to make sure you are not buying in an area that has been going through high, double digit appreciation because, unfortunately, you could be leaving yourself open to a massive decrease in value if the market makes a correction.

In my opinion, and according to Don Arceri, a licensed Illinois appraiser, it is sometimes better financially to buy in towns or areas of towns that are already established and growing. There is a better history of value there, and you have less of a chance of getting burned down the road with rapid loss of value in changing economic times. Granted, there is a certain attraction to buying a brand new home, but the downside is the financial risk you are taking as often times new construction has inflated values that may not carry into the future once a neighborhood or condo building is complete. If areas in which you are considering buying are appreciating too fast beyond the historical average, that should raise a red flag for you, so always be cautious. I will be sharing more about this later in the book.

Real estate appreciates for one reason: People need a home to live in and therefore create demand. Why is there demand?

- Our population will more than double by 2100[3]
- This increased population needs a place to live.

---

[2] Federal Housing Finance Agency, Housing Price Index, www.fhfa.gov

If our population is currently 306 million[4], according to the U.S. Census Bureau (2009 figure), we can expect that population to more than double to 700 million by 2100. This growth will stem largely from immigration to the United States[5]. From that statistic alone, we can see that there will always be a demand for housing.

Furthermore, more homes have to be built to meet the demands of our growing population. Using data from the National Association of Home Builders, I have displayed housing starts since 1997 in *Figure 2-4*. Housing starts is the number of new homes being built by home builders. This data

Figure 2-3

only refers to single-family homes. However, the Association does publish data on condos and multi-family starts as well.

You will note that in the last couple of years, the number of home starts has fallen due to the changing economy. Perhaps the builders were building too many homes too fast in prior years and the demand was no longer there as our economy began to change and people decided to stay put until things blew over.

---

[3] US Census Bureau, www.census.gov
[4] US Census Bureau, 2009 Data, www.census.gov
[5] US Census Bureau, www.census.gov

Even if there is a slowdown in housing starts, the important point to remember here is that there is demand for housing and that demand will change from year to year. The fact remains that our population is growing and people need a place to live. Therefore, building will continue, but just at a varied rate.

The number of new home starts is just one of many economic factors used in gauging the health of our economy. The government is paying attention to how many new homes builders are constructing. As a side note, when our government makes an economic announcement of new home starts, the news can actually affect mortgage rates, and the stock market can go up or down on any given day. I will talk more about interest rates later in the book.

The Reasons Real Estate Appreciates

Take a look at *Figure 2-5* and think about this: if you were paying $300,000 for a home knowing it would be worth $200,000 in 10 years, would you buy the home? Your answer would probably be no. If real estate values remained flat and your $300,000 home was worth $300,000 in 10 years, you would more than likely not want to own it because you wouldn't

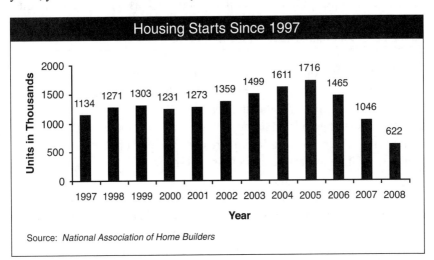

Figure 2-4

want the headaches of repairing your roof or making improvements if the value was going to be the same or less in 10 years. In that case, you would instead continue to rent and let someone else worry about those repair headaches. Over time, real estate appreciates in value, which is why you would choose Scenario 3 in *Figure 2-5*. Even in down or changing economic times with zero or negative appreciation rates, we buy homes because history shows us that values will grow over time.

Which Scenario Would You Prefer?		
Scenario 1	**Scenario 2**	**Scenario 3**
$300,000 2009	$300,000 2009	$300,000 2009
$200,000 2019	$300,000 2019	$400,000 2019
Negative Appreciation	**Break Even Appreciation**	**Positive Appreciation**

Figure 2-5

Homeowners should also make an effort to help maintain or increase their home's value. Because most homeowners take pride in owning a home, they do things that reflect that pride, such as putting in additions, making kitchen and bathroom improvements, landscaping, and other enhancements that increase the value of a home.

For example, you see two 20-year-old homes that are identical, except that one has a new kitchen and master bath; the other doesn't. Would you be willing to pay more for the updated home? Appraisers and home sales data tell us that the updated home will appraise for more than the outdated home. If you were looking for an already updated home, you most likely would be willing to pay the extra money to have that.

If you have ever been out looking at homes, you might have noticed homes that have not been updated or have horrible curb appeal tend to sit for sale longer than updated homes. The next time you're out, pick out a few homes for sale in your area that are in shabby shape and see how long they take to sell.

In summary, real estate appreciates because (1) there is demand for real estate and (2) we as homeowners add value to the land our home sits on. When I bought my second home, I purposely chose one that was not updated because my wife and I anticipated making improvements specific to our needs and tastes. In return, we paid less for the home compared to similar homes that had sold or were for sale in our neighborhood of interest. In my case, the market value of the home was less because it had not been updated and still had most of the original features from the time it was first built in 1986.

The History of Home Appreciation

In 1626, Native Americans reportedly traded or sold the island of Manhattan, New York to the Dutch for $24 in beads and trinkets. In 2008, Manhattan was worth an estimated $250 billion. Based on this $250 billion, the annual appreciation would be roughly 6.22% over 382 years. As there are bad times in recent history over the last 36 years, there have also been bad times over the last 382 years, including the Great Depression.

In *Figure 2-6* you will see that from 1976 through the end of 2008, our country has seen an average home appreciation of 5.66%. So, historically our country has had steady appreciation over time.

In viewing *Figure 2-6*, you can see that real estate does not appreciate consistently year after year. You will note in the same figure that in the early 2000s, there were some appreciation values of almost 12%. However, as you can see in *Figure 2-8*, (see page 32) the average appreciation levels for 2007 and 2008 were 1.15%. For 2009, although the year has not ended yet, the year-to-date appreciation numbers are showing that we have fallen below zero. As I mentioned a few pages earlier, you can also see by looking at *Figure 2-8* that Arizona, California, Florida, and Nevada were the leaders in negative appreciation.

Not once over the last 33 years has our country seen an average appreciation level of less than zero percent. Considering that the appreciation level was near 12% in 2004-2005, one could expect a correction to take

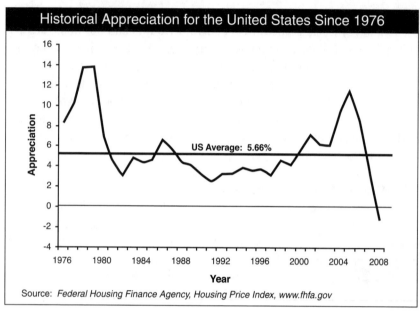

Figure 2-6

place since the historical average is 5.66%. As of this writing, a combination of factors is contributing to our economic times, and the reduction in real estate values is one of them.

Figure 2-7 illustrates the historical appreciation levels for the entire United States by state. What is interesting about this historical data is the variation of appreciation levels between states.

I personally feel the effects of the real estate market of 2007-2009. My wife and I bought our house in a Chicago suburb in March of 2006. Our house is probably not worth too much more than what we paid for it in 2006 (perhaps less), even though we have made some significant improvements. We also knew that we were in historical times regarding appreciation levels and that we could be at risk if the real estate market ever changed, which it did shortly after we bought our home. The alternative was to sit on the sidelines and continue to rent until the appreciation levels

State by State Average Real Estate Appreciation 1976-2008

Alabama	4.47%	Kentucky	4.62%	North Dakota	4.62%
Alaska	5.08%	Louisiana	4.97%	Ohio	4.43%
Arizona	6.07%	Maine	6.85%	Oklahoma	4.25%
Arkansas	4.48%	Maryland	6.86%	Oregon	6.99%
California	8.12%	Massachusetts	7.52%	Pennsylvania	5.47%
Colorado	6.09%	Michigan	4.94%	Rhode Island	7.08%
Connecticut	6.56%	Minnesota	5.85%	South Carolina	4.96%
Delaware	6.00%	Mississippi	4.09%	South Dakota	5.02%
District of Columbia	8.29%	Missouri	4.69%	Tennessee	4.72%
Florida	5.61%	Montana	6.20%	Texas	4.31%
Georgia	4.67%	Nebraska	4.34%	Utah	6.09%
Hawaii	7.86%	Nevada	5.99%	Vermont	6.11%
Idaho	5.50%	New Hampshire	7.59%	Virginia	6.06%
Illinois	5.49%	New Jersey	7.11%	Washington	7.58%
Indiana	4.40%	New Mexico	5.64%	West Virginia	4.08%
Iowa	4.42%	New York	6.85%	Wisconsin	5.19%
Kansas	4.21%	North Carolina	5.05%	Wyoming	5.72%

Average appreciation for all 50 states and District of Columbia = 5.66%

Source: *Federal Housing Finance Agency, Housing Price Index, www.fhfa.gov*

Figure 2-7

dropped off some. But this alternative wasn't ideal for us, considering that we would be missing out on the long-term financial benefits. We knew when we were buying that we did not have an interest in moving in the immediate future. In addition, because we are confident based on the fact that real estate appreciates in our country, we now know, as we did then, that our home will appreciate. When we want to sell our home down the road, we will be able to sell it for more than what we paid for it.

State by State Average Real Estate Appreciation 2007-2008

Alabama	4.34%	Kentucky	2.76%	North Dakota	5.28%
Alaska	2.62%	Louisiana	3.91%	Ohio	-0.39%
Arizona	-5.29%	Maine	1.72%	Oklahoma	4.22%
Arkansas	2.51%	Maryland	-0.92%	Oregon	2.71%
California	-10.72%	Massachusetts	-2.84%	Pennsylvania	2.34%
Colorado	1.59%	Michigan	-4.32%	Rhode Island	3.84%
Connecticut	-0.57%	Minnesota	-1.25%	South Carolina	3.94%
Delaware	0.88%	Mississippi	3.84%	South Dakota	4.39%
District of Columbia	-0.15%	Missouri	1.61%	Tennessee	3.99%
Florida	-7.65%	Montana	5.48%	Texas	4.84%
Georgia	1.90%	Nebraska	1.37%	Utah	6.98%
Hawaii	0.09%	Nevada	-10.04%	Vermont	2.40%
Idaho	3.72%	New Hampshire	1.75%	Virginia	-0.20%
Illinois	0.68%	New Jersey	-1.25%	Washington	3.72%
Indiana	1.54%	New Mexico	4.20%	West Virginia	2.43%
Iowa	2.32%	New York	0.14%	Wisconsin	1.32%
Kansas	2.40%	North Carolina	4.59%	Wyoming	7.14%

Average appreciation for all 50 states and District of Columbia = 1.15%

Source: *Federal Housing Finance Agency, Housing Price Index, www.fhfa.gov*

Figure 2-8

Now that I've explained home appreciation, you can see how appreciation levels swing widely from year to year depending on the state of our economy. Based on this, it is the long-term holding of real estate that will provide you with the most benefit in terms of increasing your net worth. Keep in mind, history has always provided for positive appreciation over time because of our growing population and subsequent demand for owning real estate.

When Is a Good Time to Buy?

Now that you can see that appreciation values go up and down, you're probably asking: When is the right time to buy? I can't tell you exactly when the right time for you to buy is. That is a decision you will have to make on your own by taking into consideration your current financial situation, where you are at in your life, and if you are willing to take advantage of good buys in your area that may result from the downturn in the economy. If you are thinking about the process, attend a homebuyer's workshop and read additional books like this one to become comfortable about owning a home. In addition, talk to a real estate agent to get a feel for home values in a specific town. Furthermore, take time out to speak with people you know who have recently become homeowners for the first time. You will then begin to feel confident in proceeding to buy a home yourself.

With the record number of foreclosures at the time of this writing, there has been an incredible opportunity to purchase a home. These foreclosed homes are often sold at a healthy discount from what their value currently is or once was. Some experts in real estate say "buy when real estate is on sale." Well, the current economic times are making the purchase of homes very attractive.

In a very recent example, my mother had been in the process of looking to purchase a new home. The same style home she was looking at last year was now selling for roughly $100,000 less in the summer of 2009. Thus, there are bargains to be had.

Let me share with you a historical example of appreciation. In the suburbs of Chicago, my parents paid $75,000 for their home in 1974 and sold it for $205,000 in 1995. That translates to a 4.91% average appreciation rate over the 21-year period in which they owned the home.

I could write about countless other examples of people who bought real estate, held it, and then later sold it for a profit. But instead, I'd rather you gain your knowledge firsthand by asking your parents and grandparents what they paid for their first home. You will be amazed at the price they tell you. If that first home is still standing, find out its current value by going to www.zillow.com, which is a website designed to provide you with an estimated value of homes. Once you know today's value, go to my website at www.whyownahome.com/thebook to use the appreciation calculator to determine the average appreciation since they bought their home.

Ultimately, however, you have to decide for yourself the best time to buy and if you're comfortable with the price you are paying in relation to historical data. I can say this: America always bounces back, and the value of our real estate has always gone up over time.

Based on my own personal experiences, those of my clients, and the analysis we will perform in a moment, I can tell you that regardless of the current appreciation levels, buying a home will financially be more beneficial than renting over the long-term. Real estate is a silent investment in that it is providing a roof over your head; as you go about your daily life, it is appreciating in value over time, thus increasing your net worth as your equity grows.

As you can see, the appreciation of real estate plays a significant role in the creation of wealth for people. Over time, you will hopefully pay off the home you live in. The good thing is, it will continue to appreciate in value when paid off. Unfortunately, at some point in life, you will no longer be in a position to maintain a home on your own and may need to downsize to a different type of home. However, as the home is being paid off and appreciation is taking place during your time of ownership, equity is accruing. When you sell the home, the proceeds may be used for other types of housing, such as a rental or ownership unit in a retirement home.

Tax Benefits of Owning

Uncle Sam—-our Federal Government—-rewards you for owning a home as per the tax code and IRS publications 936 and 530. The government allows you to deduct the following on your tax return:

- Interest paid on your home loan
- Property taxes
- Mortgage insurance, in some cases (explained later)

These tax benefits are not the foremost way to create wealth with real estate, but they can help you out significantly as a first-time homebuyer by improving your cash flow and potentially allowing you to continue to save/invest for retirement as you pay off your home loan.

The topic of tax benefits is another important area of the homebuying process that people are less familiar with, but it is a topic that they really need to understand. Realizing the importance of tax benefits will help you see how homeownership can be more affordable. Using information from the IRS tax code, in *Figure 2-9*, I have put together an example of a single man who earns $65,000 per year and is therefore in the 25% tax bracket based on IRS 2008 tax tables.

I am not a CPA (Certified Public Accountant) or a tax preparer, but I can say that based on common knowledge regarding the impact of these tax benefits, the benefit in *Figure 2-9* would be an additional $191 per month. How much more relieved would you be if you could contribute more to your retirement as a result of increased cash flow from these home-owner tax breaks?

Adjusting Your W-4 Withholding Allowance

Often times, homebuyers adjust their W-4 withholding from their pay-check so that less is taken out every month to provide more cash flow. Furthermore, that extra money every month can earn interest if placed in a savings account or if invested. That huge tax refund at the end of the year is nice, but Uncle Sam gives it to you without paying you any interest for the duration they were holding it. For this reason alone, many people adjust their W-4.

Many new homeowners will find their tax refund to be greater than the previous year if they did not adjust their W-4. The IRS at www.irs.gov has

Tax Benefits From Owning vs. Renting

A single man earning $65,000 per year with a $150,000 mortgage balance at 6.25% amortized over 30 years. Income tax bracket is 25%. State tax rates not used for this calculation since tax rates vary by state.

Renting Analysis

Annual Income		$65,000
Deductions	-	$5,450
Exemptions	-	$3,500
Adjusted Taxable Gross Income	=	**$56,050**
Taxes Paid	=	$10,363

Owning Analysis

Annual Income		$65,000
Less Interest on $150,000 Mortgage	-	$9,325
Less Property Taxes	-	$5,300
Adjusted Taxable Gross Income	=	**$46,875**
Taxes Paid	=	$8,063

Summary

Renting Taxes Paid		$10,363
Owning Taxes Paid	-	$8,063
Tax Benefit over Renting	=	**$2,300**
Your monthly cash flow from owning improves by:		**$191**

Figure 2-9

a great worksheet to help you figure out exactly what your withholding allowance should be. Your CPA / tax preparer would also be able to assist you with this.

Let me caution you about making certain decisions based on receiving tax breaks. People often think that because of tax breaks, they can buy a more expensive home than they should. Even though they qualify for the home regardless of the tax breaks, they buy too much and end up with cash flow problems. Because they have a bigger mortgage to pay, they don't save, and, therefore, are not prepared for emergencies such as job loss, illness, extended time off work, etc. Keep in mind that a bigger mortgage means you may not financially be able to make your monthly payments AND put money in savings at the same time.

My advice would be to save or invest the tax benefit you are receiving. If you buy a less expensive home, you should be able to afford to save or invest the entire tax benefit. For example, if you are receiving an extra $298 per month as a result of the tax benefit, save or invest the entire $298. As I will talk about in the next section, compound interest will make a huge impact on your long-term creation of wealth.

The Power of Compound Interest

You may wonder what the power of compound interest has to do with buying a home. Remember that the title of this book is Create Wealth with Homeownership, so you need to look at your entire financial plan in addition to owning a home. Even if you never buy a home, utilizing the power of compound interest will have a significant impact on your ability to create money to live an enjoyable retirement.

Compound interest is simply adding interest to the principal you have invested. If you never touch the principal invested or the interest added, you will continue to earn interest on top of the interest over time. So a simple $100 invested at a 6% rate of return over one year would be worth $106.16. After 30 years, that $100 investment would be worth $602.25. In this case, all you did was set $100 aside.

What if you took that original $100 and then added $100 per month to it for the next 30 years. Now, you would have $101,053.76. My bet is that you would hardly miss the $100 you set aside every month. Imagine how much you could accumulate if you kept adding to your $100 as your income grew every year?

I will tie compound interest into buying a home in the pages ahead, but for now, let's take a look at *Figure 2-10*, which illustrates how your money can grow over time by taking the $191 gained from the tax benefit in *Figure 2-9*. You will note that as the years roll by, your investment growth really accelerates as the interest is being compounded on what you have already contributed along with what you continue to contribute monthly.

As you can see, in 30 years you would have $132,563 at a conservative 4% return. But what if you waited 10 years to start saving and you only had 20 years to save prior to retirement? If you waited 10 years, you will then have invested only for 20 years, and therefore you will have earned $70,054. So let's look at *Figure 2-11*, which shows the lost opportunity cost by waiting to start saving.

By not saving those first ten years, the $22,920 that you would have put away would have cost you $39,589 in interest earned from compounding. Is that a wise trade? You can see why you want to still contribute to retirement and savings while still taking advantage of the benefits of home-ownership. The power of compound interest is so amazing that you can't ignore it. The big problem, however, is that many people don't understand compound interest or investing and, therefore, actually do ignore it.

When you enter the working world, it's very important to start a savings plan and begin to utilize the power of compound interest. If you can let your money grow for 40 to 50 years, imagine what that can do for you. The $100 we talked about at the start of this section would be worth $200,244 in 40 years if you kept adding $100 to it every month. That's almost double the money you would have from compounding for 30 years. The reverse is true as well as I pointed out in *Figure 2-11*. Let's say you waited until age 45 to start saving and let the money grow for only 20 years

Power of Compound Interest					
$191 invested monthly	**rate of return**				
	4%	**5%**	**6%**	**7%**	**8%**
5 Years	$ 12,663	$ 12,989	$ 13,326	$ 13,624	$ 14,034
10 Years	$ 28,124	$ 29,659	$ 31,301	$ 33,059	$ 34,943
15 Years	$ 47,003	$ 51,052	$ 55,546	$ 60,540	$ 66,093
20 Years	$ 70,054	$ 78,507	$ 88,250	$ 99,497	$112,503
25 Years	$ 98,199	$113,742	$132,362	$154,724	$181,646
30 Years	$132,563	$158,961	$191,862	$233,014	$284,659
35 Years	$174,523	$216,994	$272,120	$344,001	$438,131
40 Years	$225,755	$291,470	$380,775	$501,339	$666,782

Figure 2-10

before you needed to touch it. In 20 years, that $100 would be worth only $46,535 if you kept contributing $100 per month to it. That's less than half of what you would gain if you invested for 30 years.

My recommendation would be to find a reputable financial advisor who can help you establish an investment portfolio into which you can con-

Lost Opportunity by Not Saving/Investing	
Using a conservative 4% return, let's take a look at the lost opportunity cost by waiting 10 years to invest.	
Years Invested	**Value**
30 Years	$132,563
20 Years	– $70,054
Difference	= $62,509
Actual money you invested	– $22,920
Lost opportunity cost (lost interest gain) =	**$39,589**

Figure 2-11

tribute money every month. This would be separate from whatever you are contributing to your employer-sponsored 401(k) or 403(b). By working with a financial advisor, you will develop a balanced investment strategy so that you can achieve an overall greater return on your investment than you would by just sticking your money into a savings account. I will talk more about finding and using an investment advisor in Chapter 10. For now, I just want you to understand the concept of compound interest and how important of a role it plays in your ability to create money for your retirement years.

The Rent Vs. Own Analysis

Now that you are armed with an understanding of real estate appreciation, tax benefits, the power of compound interest, and some history, you should begin to understand how important the financial side of real estate is to your overall financial state in life. Using a Rent vs. Own Analysis, I will now tie together all of what I have talked about so far. This will show you exactly how wealth is created over time.

When I meet with clients for the first time, I complete this exact Rent vs. Own Analysis so they can see how their situation will be affected by the decision to purchase. Let's take a look at a renter versus an owner to see how net worth and wealth are created by owning real estate. In *Figure 2-12*, I am showing you the details of a single woman's situation. She came to see me and was hesitant about buying a home, as she had been renting since college graduation.

To illustrate her situation, I am comparing her $1,125 in rent with $15,000 in savings to buying a $180,000 condo with $10,000 down from savings, allocating $2,500 for closing costs and $1,500 for moving expenses, leaving $1,000 left in savings. I am using a 6.375% interest rate.

In a 5-year period, the net worth of the homeowner grew to $49,775 greater than that of the renter because the homeowner had many factors working in her favor:

Rent vs. Own Analysis $180,000 Condo

Cost of Renting

		Cost of Owning	
Rent	$1,100	Principal & Interest (P&I)	$1,061
Insurance	+ $25	Plus Taxes, Insurance (T&I)	+ $446
		Monthly Cost	= $1,507
		Less Tax Benefits (T)	- $316
		Less Principal Paid (P)	- $157
Net Monthly Cost=	$1,125	Net Monthly Cost	= $1,033

Owing costs less by $92

Renting Analysis

		Ownership Analysis	
5 years of rent	$70,193	5 years of PITI	$90,398
(2% annual rental increase)		Less Principal Paid	- $11,092
		Less Tax Benefit	- $18,492
Net Cost to Rent =	$70,193	Net Cost to Own	= $60,814

Owning costs less over 5 years by $9,379

Asset Accumulation

	Asset Accumulation	
Savings Account $15,000	Real Estate Value after 5 years	$218,998
Adding $150 per month	with 4% appreciation	
3% interest (rate of return)	Less Loan Balance	- $158,908
	Total Home Equity	= $60,090
	Savings Account	$1,000
	Adding $150 per month plus	
	$92 from cost of owning difference	
	3% interest (rate of return)	
Savings Balance = $27,121	Savings Balance	= $16,806
After 5 years	After 5 years	
Net Worth = $27,121	**Net Worth**	**= $76,896**
(after 5 years)	**(after 5 years)**	

Owning has greater net worth of: $49,775

Net Worth	= $41,202	Net Worth	= $157,946
(after 10 years)		(after 10 years)	

Owning has greater net worth after 10 years of: $116,745

Figure 2-12

1) The homeowner had less monthly costs as a result of tax benefits.
2) The homeowner took the $92 difference in savings from owning and added that to the $150 per month she was already saving, which was providing a very conservative 3% rate of return.
3) The homeowner experienced five years of appreciation at a conservative 4%. (Remember: the national average over the last 32 years has been 5.66%.)

Even if this homeowner chose not to buy and tried to invest her $15,000 at a higher rate of return, she would never come close to creating the net worth over five years that she would by owning a home. The $15,000 invested at 8% over five years without a monthly contribution would be $22,039. If she continued to contribute $150 monthly, she would only achieve $33,445.

Furthermore, even if we calculated the home appreciation at 2% annually, her net worth would be $110,921 in ten years, resulting in a difference of $69,720 over what she would have had from renting. This is still a significant increase in net worth, proving that homeownership is a financially feasible choice.

Assume she bought a home in 2009 and was receiving 0% appreciation. At the end of 10 years of no appreciation, her net worth would be $71,502. This is still $30,300 greater as a result of paying down principal and due to the tax benefits she received. However, as you have learned in this chapter, the economy goes through cycles and that based on history, the homebuyer in this example could expect to see positive appreciation over time.

Let's take a look at a second example in *Figure 2-13* in which the homebuyer bought a $140,000 condo instead of a $180,000 condo, and still put $10,000 down.

In this example, when buying a less expensive home, this borrower was able to contribute more to savings. Because of the power of compound interest, this homeowner would have a greater net worth than if she had bought a more expensive home.

Rent vs. Own Analysis $140,000 Condo

Cost of Renting		**Cost of Owning**	
Rent	$1,100	Principal & Interest (P&I)	$811
Insurance	+ $25	Plus Taxes, Insurance (T&I)	+ $359
		Monthly Cost	= $1,170
		Less Tax Benefits (T)	- $255
		Less Principal Paid (P)	- $120
Net Monthly Cost =	$1,125	Net Monthly Cost	= $795

Owing costs less by $330

Renting Analysis		**Ownership Analysis**	
5 years of rent	$70,193	5 years of PITI	$70,202
(2% annual rental increase)		Less Principal Paid	- $8,482
		Less Tax Benefit	- $14,907
Net Cost to Rent =	$70,193	Net Cost to Own	= $46,773

Owning costs less over 5 years by $23,420

Asset Accumulation		**Asset Accumulation**	
Savings Account $15,000		Real Estate Value after 5 years	$170,331
Adding $150 per month		with 4% appreciation	
3% interest (rate of return)		Less Loan Balance	- $121,518
		Total Home Equity	= $77,217
		Savings Account	$1,000
		Adding $150 per month plus	
		$92 from cost of owning difference	
		3% interest (rate of return)	
Savings Balance =	$27,121	Savings Balance	= $32,192
After 5 years		After 5 years	
Net Worth =	**$27,121**	**Net Worth**	= **$109,409**
(after 5 years)		**(after 5 years)**	

Owning has greater net worth of: $82,288

Net Worth =	$41,202	Net Worth	= $225,008
(after 10 years)		(after 10 years)	

Owning has greater net worth after 10 years of: $183,806

Figure 2-13

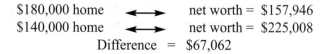

$180,000 home   ⟷   net worth = $157,946
$140,000 home   ⟷   net worth = $225,008
Difference = $67,062

From *Figures 2-12* and *2-13*, you can easily see now how wealth is created with homeownership. The simple facts that real estate appreciates and that you receive tax benefits for owning make homeownership financially rewarding over time. When you contribute to savings along with taking advantage of the benefits of homeownership, the power of compound interest begins to work in your favor, thus increasing your net worth.

The lesser expensive condo provided for significant monthly savings over that of the more expensive condo. The $180,000 condo provided $92 in monthly savings, while the $140,000 condo provided a $330 monthly savings. When you added the $330 to the $150 already being saved with the lesser expensive condo, the power of compound interest really went to work, accelerating the creation of wealth.

Unfortunately, many homebuyers ignore these crucial financial concepts. Oddly enough, they choose not to become educated about them. Furthermore, most mortgage professionals do not share this information with potential homebuyers. This is why you need to find and work with a mortgage professional who believes that client education comes first. I will be sharing with you in Chapter 5 on how to find a good mortgage professional to work with.

My hope is that from reading this chapter you are beginning to really think twice about money and the decision you make regarding your use of it. Furthermore, I hope you now see that homeownership combined with continual saving and investing is crucial to your long-term financial success.

CHAPTER 3
First-Time Homebuyers

Assuming you are a first-time homebuyer, purchasing a home is probably going to be the biggest and most nerve-racking event of your life to date. There will be so many unknowns, but I hope to clear them up for you with this book. As you go through the process of buying a home, make sure to keep an open mind and choose good professionals with whom to work. By having trustworthy professionals working on your behalf, you will find the process of buying your first home a lot less stressful.

In this chapter, I will share some ideas to ease some concerns you might have as a first-time homebuyer.

One of my clients, Melony, never thought she could afford a home of her own. She was a single mother of three girls who had been living in a two-bedroom apartment for over five years and sharing a room with one of her daughters. During my initial meeting with her, she shared some basic numbers with me, and I advised her that she would indeed be in the position to buy a home.

To help Melony understand the homebuying process better, I gave her a copy of my first-time homebuyers' manual, which was a 20-page version of this book. Within two months she called me back and wanted to start the process. We got together in my office to discuss her situation. During our meeting, I was able to officially pre-approve her, about which she could not have been more excited. Her next step was to go off "shopping" for a home with a real estate agent and she luckily found the perfect home almost immediately. At the closing a few months later, she had tears in her eyes as she could not believe she was in the final step to owning her own home. The experience was both overwhelming and uplifting for her; it was also rewarding for me as I am always pleased to see the happiness of a first-time homebuyer. I asked her at the closing why she had waited so long to buy a home. (She could have definitely qualified a few years earlier.) She responded simply that she didn't think she would qualify.

In Melony's case, she took the time to learn and seek out good professionals with whom to work. By reading this book, you are doing the same. The information you will learn from this book and others like it will make a significant difference in how this first homebuying transaction will be for you, not to mention how your experience will be as a lifetime owner of homes.

Having a pleasant and smooth buying experience will depend on whom you choose as a mortgage professional as well as the real estate agent you are using to find a home. Take your time to ask the appropriate questions, which I will cover later in Part 2.

Don't Overbuy

I have said this before: don't overbuy or buy outside of your means. The biggest mistake first-time homebuyers can make is buying too much home and then finding themselves strapped for cash because the mortgage payment is so much larger than the rent they had been paying. Look for a home that is going to be equal to or slightly higher than what you are currently paying in rent. This will allow you to comfortably transition from renting to owning so you are able to continue to save and fund retirement accounts. Remind yourself of the Rent vs. Own Analysis in Chapter 2. The creation of net worth is created more quickly by owing and saving at the same time.

Many people who want to buy a home are financially responsible and know how to manage their finances, yet sometimes they lack good decision-making skills in terms of the type of home they want to live in. Smart people can still often get in way over their heads when they have bought too much home and then start having trouble meeting their obligations.

Here is what can happen when you buy too much home:

▼ You want to fill it with furniture.
▼ You want to improve it.
▼ You rack up a lot of credit card debt furnishing and improving.

▼ You have an unexpected and expensive home repair or medical expense.

▼ You end up with huge cash flow problems.

▼ You can't pay your mortgage.

▼ You end up behind in payments.

▼ Your credit score drops.

▼ Now you can't refinance because your credit is bad.

▼ You are forced to sell the home or be kicked out because the bank took it back in foreclosure. You thus lose whatever equity you had in the home.

▼ Now you can't qualify to buy a home for at least another four years.

▼ **Now you are in a financial mess.**

Figure 3-1 illustrates how this disaster plays out in terms of cash flow from a numerical point of view. I have left the loan amount out of this example.

Cash Flow Problems From Buying Too Much Home		
Monthly Income		$6,250
Car Payment	-	$391
Credit Cards	-	$0
Housing Allocation	-	$1,708
Estimated Taxes	-	$2,053
Cash Flow Left	=	**$1,526**

Now add $200 per month to your payments from credit card debt you racked up after buying this new home:

Cash Flow Left		$1,526
Less Monthly Credit Card Payments	-	$200
Cash Flow Left	=	**$1,326**

Figure 3-1

You might say, "I can live on $1,326 per month for food, entertainment, utility bills, insurance, cell phone bills, etc." But can you still contribute to savings / retirement every month on $1,326 left over? What if you went out and charged up $5,000 in credit card debt on two different cards buying new furniture, etc.?

But you say, "No problem. I can handle the $100 per month forever," and then you charge more because you want new drapes, a new bed, new clothes, etc. Now the $5,000 debt becomes $10,000.

As you watch your cash flow disappear into credit card payments, you find that things are getting harder financially. Furthermore, this racked-up debt is now stressing you out. You want to pay it off, but you don't have the cash flow to do it. You stop putting money into savings so that you can live. One little setback with a medical bill or an unexpected car repair could push you over the edge with no money left over on a given month.

In *Figure 3-2*, take a look at the cash flow when you buy a less expensive home with a loan amount of $140,000. The lower loan amount provides for an increase in cash flow from the *Figure 3-1* amount of $296 per month. In this example, the housing allocation has been reduced to $1,412 per month because of the lower loan amount.

Cash Flow Problems From Buying Less Expensive Home		
Monthly Income		$6,250
Car Payment	-	$391
Credit Cards	-	$0
Housing Allocation	-	$1,412
Estimated Taxes	-	$2,053
Cash Flow Left	=	**$1,822**

Figure 3-2

In my opinion, an extra $296 per month can do a lot.   In this case, rather than charging a new couch, you could use the extra cash flow to save so that you can buy that new couch you wanted by paying for it in cash. You can also easily and comfortably contribute to savings and retirement accounts with an extra $296 per month and build your emergency fund as well. Just remember the power of compound interest that we discussed in Chapter 2 with *Figure 2-9* in which $191 per month turned into $132,563 over 30 years at a 4% rate of return . With the lesser expensive home and less credit card debt, you can easily contribute $100-$200 per month to a savings investment plan and still have money left over to live a comfortable lifestyle.

As a first-time homebuyer, I myself fell into this trap because I purchased too much home. I had no money left over to buy furniture. What does a single 30-year-old guy need with a 3-bedroom townhouse with a full basement and a 2-car garage? I would have been better off starting out in a much smaller townhouse or condo. Like many people, I was focused on the wrong part of the equation I referred to in *Figure 1-1*. I looked at the personal side and not the financial side and, as a result, bought way too much house for my situation at the time.

Even though you may qualify to buy a more expensive home, the question is, do you really need it? See how the difference in a $40,000 less expensive loan impacts your monthly cash flow? You can see how charging credit cards can begin to severely impact your cash flow as well. Also, remember the power of compound interest. Always think about what your money can do for you if it's working for you. If you blow your money on too much housing and other things, you will not have money working for you generating interest. You will be house rich, but cash poor.

The Early 2000s

At the time of this writing, our country was experiencing record foreclosures. For a brief period in the early 2000s, people were able to buy a home with little or no money down and with bad credit. These buyers never did anything to improve their credit once they were able to buy, and because of their bad habits (such as overspending), they found themselves with no other option than to give up their home to foreclosure.

As I will talk about later, loan programs still exist for people with less-than-perfect credit, but the terms of such loans prevent most people from buying outside their means. If you fall into the less-than-perfect credit category, you still have the potential to purchase a home if you qualify, but if you do, this is your chance to work hard as having a mortgage on your credit report will help improve your credit scores significantly. You will learn more about credit in Chapter 6.

My intention is not to scare you; I only want to caution you that when you make this first step into homeownership, you do it the right way so you are able to take advantage of the financial benefits it is intended to provide you.

Qualifying for a huge payment does not mean you want to have that much payment. Even when you buy, you should still want to continue to save and contribute to your retirement accounts. So, again, starting out in a smaller home with a payment equal to or slightly higher than what you are paying for rent would be a good start.

Your Parents and Grandparents Think Differently

Keep in mind that when your parents bought their first home, times were different as they learned from their parents, who definitely had a different view of money. Looking back to just before the Great Depression in the 1920s, mortgages contained a clause that stated the bank could call you up and demand that within 30 days, you pay your mortgage balance off. Well, people did not have that kind of money around and found themselves losing their homes during that time when the banks needed money back as a result of the stock market crash on October 29, 1929. Many people ended up losing their homes; therefore, the goal became owning a home outright rather than just carrying a mortgage. In celebration of paying off the mortgage, people in those days had mortgage burning parties. Yet, I'm sure plenty of people have such parties today as paying off a home is a huge accomplishment.

Since the Great Depression, new laws have been enacted to prevent a bank from calling your loan due. The only thing a bank can do is demand that you make your monthly payment. Therefore, the way a mortgage is viewed today is significantly different than how it was viewed decades ago. So I caution you when considering the advice of family and friends as their circumstances for borrowing money either in the past or in the present may be very different from yours. Often times, their decisions were not based on mathematics or financial planning but on the "it's what you're supposed to do" mentality.

I'm not saying that you shouldn't run ideas by your circle of influence and get their feedback, but your mortgage professional will present more accurate and unbiased plans and solutions as they apply to your personal financial situation based on current lending practices. I do recommend, however, that you talk with peers who are buying homes for the first time as well and see what type of loan programs they are getting. Remember, each person is in a different set of circumstances regarding their home purchase, so their overall choices may not be the same as yours. Once you have met with a mortgage professional and developed a plan, then take the time to share that plan with those advising you so you can explain to them why you're doing what you're doing.

Developing a Strategy in the Homebuying Process

Strategy is very important when buying a home, especially your first home. For example, Brett came to me with the hopes of buying a condo in the city of Chicago. He wanted a two-bedroom condo and was planning to have a roommate to help him pay the mortgage every month. Because his income did not support a traditional 30-year fixed rate mortgage, I structured the loan in such a way that would allow him to qualify. Lenders do not take into consideration that you are going to have a roommate paying rent to you. A roommate's income cannot be counted because the roommate is not being used to qualify for the loan.

In this case, I structured a 5-year interest-only ARM. (Interest-only means just that; you are only paying interest on the borrowed money. You are not paying any money toward the mortgage balance to pay it down.) Since you are not paying any principal toward the balance, your monthly payment will be lower. This strategy reduced his monthly payment by $213, which then allowed him to qualify for the loan. His income would not support any other type of loan.

Had he been buying this condo for only himself, he would have been buying too much condo considering an interest-only loan was the only loan type for which he would qualify. However, taking into consideration that he was going to have a roommate paying $850 per month, this was a financially smart home purchase. Why? He was able to afford a home in an up-and-coming area of Chicago. Over time, Brett might get married, and when he does, he will be able to replace the income from the renter with that of his new spouse. He also will have the second bedroom available if he and his new spouse decide to start a family. Overall, this purchase will allow him to stay awhile in this location without incurring any costs to move in the future should his circumstances change.

After a year had passed, Brett's income was up and interest rates had fallen. I restructured the loan for Brett into a 30-year fixed rate loan at a lower interest rate. He now automatically has part of his payment being paid toward the principal to help pay down his mortgage.

As you can see, it is very important to sit down and discuss your situation fully with an experienced mortgage professional so that your circumstances for borrowing money can be completely understood and evaluated. Every individual buying for the first time is going to have different circumstances that need to be accounted for so that a personalized strategy can be developed. I will talk about how to find a mortgage professional in Part 2. In considering your purchase of a home, you should ask yourself some questions to help insure you buy a home that is going to be right for you now and in the near future:

- Will this home fit my needs in five years?
- Can I afford this mortgage and save at the same time?

- What will be happening in my life during the next five years that might require me to move?
- Will I need more space in the next five years?
- If I take on a roommate, can I afford the mortgage payment if the roommate stops paying or suddenly decides to move out?
- If I have to take on another roommate, will it be easy for me to find a replacement if need be?
- Is the area, city, or neighborhood I am considering growing or declining?
- What is going on in the area, city, or neighborhood during the next five years? For example, does the city have a growth plan, are companies moving in, is there a steady population growth, etc.?
- Do I have money in reserve to cover major repair expenses if I buy a house rather than a condo or townhouse?
- Do I want to handle the upkeep of a house, which I would not have if I owned a condo or townhouse?

Your answers to these questions will help you better define the location and type of home you choose to purchase.

The following people can help you answer these questions by providing you with important information:

- Knowledgeable real estate agents based in the town of your choice.
- City/village representatives who can give you an idea of their plans for the town.
- Local chambers of commerce , which always have a good feel for what is happening in their community.
- Association boards, if you are looking at condos / townhouses.
- Older adults in the community (they seem best tuned in to the local buzz).

Have a Financial Strategy When You Buy Your First Home

Based on the experiences of my clients and discussions with others in my profession, more than likely, you will refinance your home within two to four years of your initial purchase. A variety of factors will be in place for a refinance. Such factors include the following:

- The market changes and interest rates go down, thus lowering your payment.
- Your income goes up, changing the loan type you qualify for.
- Your home appreciates in value, changing the loan type you qualify for.
- Loan programs that might lower your payment become available.
- Your credit improves so that you can qualify for a loan with a lower interest rate.

As my client Brett did, you want to take these factors into consideration during the process of taking out your new loan so that once you take possession of your new home, you are working with the plan you and your mortgage professional have laid out.

Keep in mind that there are mortgage professionals who will complete your loan, and you will never hear from them again. However, there are those professionals who will closely work with you to ensure your new loan is right for you now and will continue to watch your loan over time, always making sure you are in the best position your circumstances and the market will allow.

Making a Budget

As a first-time homebuyer, you want to be certain that you can afford a home, so now is a good time to make a budget. Sit down and make note of where all your money is going every month. Hopefully, you have extra money left over at the end of each month. Keeping track of how you're spending money is a big step toward creating good financial habits.

To keep track of my spending, I use Quicken. This computer program provides me detailed analyses of where my money is going and helps me budget every month. With the budget, I am then able to cut back in areas in which I might be overspending so that I can contribute more money to savings. You can find Quicken at most office supply stores or online at www.quicken.com.

In making a budget, you will begin to see how in certain areas you might be overspending money that could be put to better use. You may notice that you are spending too much on entertainment or eating out. By cutting back on some of these activities, you can save a lot more money each month. My suggestion is to get a receipt for everything you purchase and to keep track of all purchases. Create a spreadsheet similar to the budget in Figure 3-3 and start logging everything you spend money on, including the basics (utilities, rent, car payment, and insurance). Also include the incidentals such as cigarettes, bottles of pop/water, vending machine snacks at work, your daily latte—everything you pay for.

When you do this, you will be amazed to discover how much you actually spend on what one may consider to be small purchases. Using this method, my wife and I discovered over $400 every month that we could cut out from wasted spending. As a result, we now plan our purchases up-front by buying in bulk and shopping smart. We cut back on eating out, and we plan our shopping trips so that we are not running out for just one item several days a week. We make one trip each month to the wholesale warehouse (Costco, Sam's, BJ's Wholesale) and one trip to a discount store to purchase our "staples." If you are single, you can benefit by shopping at a wholesale warehouse too by sharing the membership fee and bulk purchases with a friend.

You can also save a significant amount of money when bringing your own beverage to work instead of buying one from the vending machine. Do the same for lunches and snacks and you will soon see the extra money adding up in your bank account. If you purchased one bottle of water at the vending machine for $1.25 per day, based on a 5 day work week and your cost of $0.17 per bottle, you could save $21.60 per month by bringing your own.

I could go on with countless examples of how to cut back your spending, but there are other books that can teach you how to penny-pinch and save by making minor changes in your lifestyle. My point here is that cutting back can help you to improve your cash flow and net worth, and by living a financially responsible life, you will certainly further accelerate your ability to own a home, save for retirement, and live comfortably.

In *Figure 3-3*, I have provided you with a worksheet that you can use to make your own budget. On the left side is a sample budget for a single woman earning $45,000 per year who is in the 25% tax bracket, and her monthly income has been adjusted to show what she is taking home after taxes. The right side is for you to lay out your budget. You can also download a full-sized worksheet to use from my website, www.whyownahome. com/info.

In this example budget in *Figure 3-3*, the individual has $308 left per month to save and invest for retirement. I did not show it in this example, but ideally this individual would contribute some of their pre-tax income to his/her employer-sponsored 401(k), 403(b), or other similar type of retirement account. If so, this money would be taken out of the paycheck pre-tax, and, therefore, there would be a slight decrease in the take-home pay.

As you begin to track your spending and develop a budget, you will soon discover that having a monthly mortgage payment that is close to your current monthly rent payment will create less of a financial dent in your pocketbook while you gain all of the benefits of homeownership. For example, you may be comfortable spending $200 more per month for owning, whereas some may feel comfortable spending only $100 more. As I showed you in the Rent vs. Own Analysis in Chapter 2, when buying a less expensive home, which provides for a lower monthly payment, you will create wealth over time with your home and still be able to continue to con-

Making A Budget

Monthly Income		**Monthly Income**	
Your Take Home Income	$2,812	Your Income	_____
Spouse Income	$0	Spouse Income	_____
Part Time Income	$0	Part Time Income	_____
Other Income	$0	Other Income	_____
Total Income	$2,812	Total Income	_____

Monthly Expenses		**Monthly Expenses**	
Car Payment #1	$199	Car Payment #1	_____
Car Payment #2	$0	Car Payment #2	_____
Auto Insurance	$65	Auto Insurance	_____
Fuel	$150	Fuel	_____
Life Insurance	$10	Life Insurance	_____
Cell Phone	$65	Cell Phone	_____
Home Phone	$65	Home Phone	_____
Electric Bill	$45	Electric Bill	_____
Gas Bill	$45	Gas Bill	_____
Water / Sewage	$15	Water / Sewage	_____
Internet Access	$50	Internet Access	_____
Cable / Satellite	$50	Cable / Satellite	_____
Groceries	$400	Groceries	_____
Entertainment	$300	Entertainment	_____
Student Loans	$145	Student Loans	_____
Other		Other	_____
Other		Other	_____
Other		Other	_____

Total Expenses	**$1,604**	**Total Expenses**	_____
Monthly Rent	$900	Monthly Rent	_____
Total Monthly Outlay	**$2,504**	**Total Monthly Outlay**	
Subtracted from income		Subtracted from income	
Money Left	**$308**	**Money Left**	_____

Printable version of this budget is available from www.whyownahome.com/info

Figure 3-3

tribute to your retirement and savings accounts. In the end, you have to decide for yourself where your comfort level is.

Applying The Financial Side to This Example

Again, the budget in *Figure 3-3* is for a woman who earns $45,000 per year. Assuming she had a loan amount of $125,000, her housing and tax payments would be $900 per month, which is exactly the same as the $900 per month she has been paying in rent.

Using the tax tables from the IRS, I have determined she is in the 25% tax bracket. By owning a home, she will reduce her taxable income by $7,458 in the first year of owning because she can deduct the interest she pays on her mortgage. This benefit translates to a monthly improvement in cash flow by $267, based on her tax bracket.

In the budget we figured she had $308 left at the end of the month to put toward savings, investments, or living expenses, but now she will have $575 extra every month, which will make setting money aside to take advantage of the power of compound interest for retirement that much easier.

Presuming she was not saving any of the $308 per month, she now has $267 per month that she can invest as a result of owning. With the power of compound interest at a 5% rate of return, in 30 years the invested $267 per month will be worth $223,405. To further add to her net worth, if she lived in her home for 30 years, her home would be completely paid off and be worth $327,680, assuming a conservative appreciation rate of 3%. That is a combined net worth of $551,085.

We can also presume that her income will go up over time and that she will hopefully contribute more to her investment portfolio, ultimately creating a greater net worth. We can also presume that she will likely not live in the same home for 30 years. (I used the 30 years in the example, however, to demonstrate the power of money once again). Finally, we did not figure in this example the additional cash flow from tax benefits she would receive from deducting her property taxes and mortgage insurance.

As you can see from this example, buying a home can be financially beneficial for a single person earning a moderate income. Going from renting to owning will allow this homebuyer to create significant wealth over time, wealth that she would have not been able to create by renting.

As a first-time homebuyer, you need to understand why buying a home is beneficial for your pocketbook, your savings, and your investments. Tax benefits and compound interest are primary reasons for homeownership—this is the financial side of owning a home. Once you attain a good understanding of this financial side, you will see your home as more than just four walls and a roof; you will see it as a lucrative tool.

CHAPTER 4
Thinking About Future Moves / Moving Up

You may be wondering why in this chapter I'm talking about moving before you have even bought your first home. Since planning is important in helping to create wealth with homeownership, it's crucial that you think about future moves when buying your first home.

Although formal research about first-time homebuyers does not exist, I've observed (and so have colleagues in my profession) that the majority of first-timers will move within the first five to seven years of owning their first home. Those same homeowners will move into their next home where, according to the Census Bureau, they will live for an average of 14 years. (On a side note, I just recently attended a closing for a client who was buying a home from a couple who had lived in their home for 52 years. Depending on your life plans, you could very well be living in your second or third home for a period longer than 14 years.) In considering another statistic, per 2008 research from the National Association of Realtors, the average time you will own a home is 10 years. As you can see, our society is mobile, which is worth thinking about up front.

When you do decide to move, you may be moving from a condo to a townhouse or from a condo to a single-family home. You may be moving from a smaller house to a bigger house, but the two essential reasons that people desire to move into a bigger home are:

- Their income has increased, and/or
- Their family has grown, so they need more space.

There are other reasons people move including job transfers, loss of income, or downsizing. The most impractical reason that people move up is that they are trying to keep up appearances, i.e., they want to look successful by living in a big home they really can't afford.

I talked about possible job transfers earlier, but I want to emphasize here that if you know there might be a chance of moving because of a job transfer in the next two to three years, buying may not be the right decision if you will not receive money to cover the relocation expenses.

Unfortunately, many people do experience a loss of income some time in their lives either from layoffs, a family emergency, or a medical issue that prevents the person from working. My advice here goes back to what I said earlier: do not buy too much home so that your savings can sustain your housing payment (you should have 8-10 months' worth of expenses saved) should you lose a primary income. You should also make sure that you have the proper disability insurance coverage to provide you with income in the event of a disability or an injury. You would be surprised at the number of people who do not have such insurance. Many employers offer this insurance, which can be taken out of your paycheck. You can also obtain the insurance on your own. I will be talking more about insurance coverage to protect your assets in Chapter 10.

Taking into account the reasons for moving, you should now understand why it is very important to have a strategy before you purchase your first home. In addition to the fact that you will move within five to seven years of purchasing your first home, research from the US Census Bureau and the National Association of Realtors say you will move three to five times in your life, not to mention completing five to eight refinance transactions. Considering these facts, keep in mind that planning well in advance is important to your overall mortgage strategy.

Whatever the reasons for moving into a bigger home, it is essential that you manage your first home properly. Proper care of the financial side of your first home will allow you to transition into a bigger home with much more ease. A bigger home is going to require that you have more income in order to qualify, to make a larger payment, and, in some cases, to put more money down.

We are not able to predict our future, but many of us have a rough idea of what we want for our life (getting married, having a family, etc.) Keeping these goals in mind will help you plan your next moves wisely.

Furthermore, many of us have an idea of the career path we are taking and of how much our income is going to increase over time. Whether you are a young professional climbing the ranks within a company or a person starting out in a trade, you will more than likely see your income increase. At a certain point, you might want a different home for you or your family to live in, and your higher income is going to help make that possible.

Cost of Moving

In Chapter 1, I touched a little on the cost of moving. Let's take a look at the cost of moving again in relation to moving up to a bigger home. *Figure 4-1* shows the basic costs of selling a home and the break-even price. A real estate agent typically charges 5-6% commission to sell your home. Moving expenses can range from $200 to $2,500 (or more) depending on whether you move yourself or hire movers.

Cost of Moving		
Analysis if selling home for $200,000		
Sales Price		$200,000
6% real estate commission	−	$12,000
Moving expenses	−	$2,500
Total Costs	=	**$14,500**
Appreciation required to break even		$14,500
Purchase price of home should have been		**$185,500**

Figure 4-1

In looking at this example in *Figure 4-1*, you will see that in order to break even on the sale of this home, you would have had to have paid $185,500 for it. Assuming you were moving in five years of buying this home, you would have needed to see an annual appreciation level of roughly 1.52% for this move to make sound financial sense. Naturally, our hope when buying a home is that it will appreciate greater than 1.52% on average over time. Looking back at the historical national average of 5.66% that we talked about in Chapter 2, exceeding 1.52% would be possible. However, you must consider what is going on in the current real estate market in your area when thinking this through. At the time of this writing, home values were essentially flat in that some areas of our country were seeing minimal or zero appreciation levels while others were seeing negative appreciation levels.

Planning Ahead: The Numbers

If you buy a home today, and you know in four years you will want to move to a bigger home, you know you will have to either save more money for a larger down payment on the bigger home or plan on staying in your current home long enough to gain enough appreciation to use for a down payment on the new, bigger home.

In the next few examples, I will be sharing with you different analyses so you can see the future values of real estate and the costs of selling.

In this example, I am going to consider that you buy a home by yourself. In the next few years, you get married and start a family. By the sixth year, the second child is on the way and you want to move from your 2-bedroom condo to a 3-bedroom single-family home with a yard. Because you read this book and educated yourself, you have made a mental note of what the cost of a 3-bedroom single-family home is. You know that type of home is going to cost somewhere between $280,000 and $350,000, based on an annual appreciation rate of 2.5%. Let's take a look at how this plays out in *Figure 4-2*.

Assuming you are not able to sell the home on your own and will have to pay a real estate commission of 6%, you would reach your break-even point in year 3 if you needed to sell. However, if you wanted to move up to a bigger home and wanted to use some of the gain from appreciation, after six years you would have a $25,555 equity gain from appreciation. To be realistic, you only get $180,000 for the sale of your home, so let's

Annualized Appreciation Estimates

Assumptions: $160,000 Purchase Price & 2.5% appreciation rate

Year 1	$164,000	Year 4	$176,610
Year 2	$168,100	Year 5	$181,025
Year 3	$172,302	Year 6	$185,555

Estimated equity gain after 6 years of ownership: $25,555
Average gain per year over 6 years: $4,259

Figure 4-2

Calculating Your Cash For New Down Payment

Assumption: 2.5% Appreciation

Sales price of home		$180,000
Less mortgage balance	–	$129,932
Less 6% real estate commission	–	$10,800
Cash available for down payment	**=**	**$39,268**

Figure 4-3

calculate the cash you will receive from the sale to use as a down payment on your new home (in *Figure 4.3*).

In this scenario, you would have $39,268 to use as a down payment on your new home. If you were going to put 10% down and could qualify for the monthly payment, you could purchase a home valued at $392,680.

At the same time you calculate the cash you would have available for a down payment, you would want to calculate your profit on the home, as I show in *Figure 4-4*. The reason you want to calculate your profit is simply to see if you really made money on your home. It's one thing to see how much cash you will receive from the sale of your home, but when you consider improvements you put into your home and the expenses that go along with selling a home and moving, you would at the same time want to know if you turned a profit. Your profit would consist of appreciation, less improvements and cost of selling.

Calculating Your Profit From Sale Of Your Home		
Assumption: 2.5% Appreciation		
Sales price of home		$180,000
Less purchase price	–	$160,000
Less 6% real estate commission	–	$10,800
Les improvements	–	$5,200
Your profit from selling the home =		**$4,000**

Figure 4-4

As you can see in this example, you would turn a $4,000 profit on this home after improvements and real estate commission. To you, $4,000 may not sound like very munch, but keep in mind that you are moving up to a bigger home in which you may live longer and that you would receive six years' worth of an improvement in cash flow as a result of the tax benefits owning your home provides you.

In this example, I used a very conservative real estate appreciation figure of 2.5%. Considering the historical average is 5.66% for the last 32 years, let's presume in *Figure 4-5* you earned a 4% appreciation rate. After six years, your home appreciates to $202,451. Considering the market is strong when you go to sell your home, let us assume you sell your home for $200,000.

As you can see in *Figure 4-5* and *Figure 4-6*, that 1.5% increase to 4% appreciation makes a big difference. Considering what is taking place in the real estate market at the time you are wanting to sell will ultimately change your cash for down payment and your profit. When contemplating

Calculating Your Cash For New Down Payment		
Assumption: 2.5% Appreciation		
Sales price of home		$200,000
Less mortgage balance	−	$129,932
Less 6% real estate commission	−	$12,800
Cash available for down payment **=**		**$58,608**

Figure 4-5

Calculating Your Profit From Sale Of Your Home		
Assumption: 4% Appreciation		
Sales price of home		$200,000
Less purchase price	−	$160,000
Less 6% real estate commission	−	$12,800
Les improvements	−	$5,200
Your profit from selling the home **=**		**$22,800**

Figure 4-6

moving up to a bigger home in the future, remember that the equity you gain is going to play a big part in your ability to move up.

Now, let's assume appreciation was only 1.5% instead of 2.5%. This means that you will have gained less in equity to put down on the new home and, therefore, you would have to take from savings to be able to purchase the new home. Once again, because you educated yourself, you knew that you would need money in the future, and so allocated part of your savings for this very purpose.

Something to bear in mind with these scenarios is that loan programs can change over time. Let's say you have to put 20% down now, as 10%

or 15% down programs no longer exist. This change could mean that you would have to continue to live in your current home for a longer period or you would have to move farther away from a larger city to find a more affordable home. However, your expenses from commuting further to work might increase, and you might have less time to spend with your family because of the longer commute, thus affecting your quality of life.

My client Brett thought about his future needs when buying his home. He knew that he had enough friends that he would not have a problem finding a good roommate who could help pay his mortgage every month. Because the cost of a 2-bedroom condo was not that much more than a 1-bedroom condo, the income he would receive from his roommate would be more than enough to cover the difference in cost. I realize this situation is not ideal for everyone, including me. I'm not a big fan of having roommates; however, Brett knew what he was comfortable with and considered it when making his buying decision. As I previously said, the decision that Brett made let him stay in one location longer, allowing appreciation and the payment of principal to work in his favor. Ultimately, this reduces the cost of owning since he does not need to pay fees to sell one home in order to move into a bigger home in the near future.

I could describe so many more scenarios, but I will only reiterate here that you need to keep the future in mind when buying a home.

In short, plan, plan, plan. Planning is the key to creating wealth in real estate. Why? Because you need a plan to manage your financial life to be able to move up to a bigger home. The reason many people do not plan is that they do not understand money or financial concepts. My best advice would be: don't wing it.

So, let's get back to buying your first home by moving to Part 2 of this book, which focuses on the process of purchasing a home.

PART II

THE HOME BUYING PROCESS

As you read about the process of buying a home over the next few chapters, follow the graphic, which summarizes each step of the process.

CHAPTER 5
Qualifying to Buy a Home

Pre-qualifying to buy a home is an informal process of finding out how much home you can afford to buy. Pre-qualifying for a mortgage is important because it gives you an estimate of the price of the home you can afford and of how much money you will need for the down payment and closing costs. In addition, it helps you define your budgeting goals and lets you come up with some approximate numbers without the mortgage professional's needing to pull a copy of your credit report. Keep in mind that this process does not guarantee you a loan. In essence, you will sit down with a mortgage professional and provide him/her with the following information:

- Your current income
- An estimate of your current debts
- An estimate of your current savings/investments.

With this information, the mortgage professional will be able to provide you with a ballpark figure of how much home you can afford to buy. This estimate will come from figuring out how much of a monthly payment you can afford to make. But even after you figure out this estimate, don't rush to make any buying decisions! You don't want to start shopping for your home just yet.

The next step after getting pre-qualified is to get pre-approved. The difference between pre-qualification and pre-approval is that pre-qualification is, as I just described, a quick, informal process. Pre-approval, on the other hand, is a formal process whereby a copy of your credit report is viewed by a mortgage professional to determine your creditworthiness. At the same time, you will complete a loan application with the mortgage professional so that a determination can be made if you can buy a home and if so, how much of a loan you can afford. Once pre-approved, you can then seriously begin searching for a home to purchase. I will be talking about the pre-approval process in Chapter 7.

In this chapter I will show you how to determine on your own an estimate of how much home you can afford to buy before visiting a mortgage professional.

What Makes Up a Housing Payment?

So far in this book I have referred to the terms principal, interest, taxes, and insurance in different ways. You may have an idea about what these terms mean, but at this point you need to have a clearer understanding of them. Principal, Interest, Taxes, and Insurance, or PITI, refers to the four parts that make up your monthly mortgage payment.

Here is a brief description of each part:

Principal (P)	The portion of the monthly payment that is allocated to pay down your mortgage balance. (The principal is the total amount of money you borrowed.)
Interest (I)	The portion of the monthly payment allocated for interest. (The interest is the cost to borrow the principal.)
Taxes (T)	The portion of the monthly payment allocated for your property taxes. (Typically, it is the cost of your annual property taxes divided by 12.)
Insurance (I)	The portion of the monthly payment allocated for your homeowner's insurance. (Typically, it is the cost of your annual policy divided by 12.)

Figure 5-1 shows the numerical breakdown of an example PITI so you can see how your monthly payment is divided up.

In addition to the PITI in *Figure 5-1*, you could be responsible for a couple of other costs related to your monthly housing expense:

Mortgage Insurance (MI or PMI)
When you put less than 20% down on a home, you will have mortgage

Breakdown Of A Monthly Mortgage Payment (PITI)		
Principal		$137
Interest	+	$1,234
Taxes	+	$229
Insurance	+	$87
Monthly Payment	=	**$1,687**

Figure 5-1

insurance to pay as part of your monthly payment to the lender. (Mortgage insurance is described in more detail in the pages ahead).

Homeowner's Association (HOA) Dues

This is the monthly amount required by the homeowner's association. Typically you pay HOA dues when buying a home that has an association such as a condo or townhouse. You pay this separately to the HOA if you live in a home that requires such dues.

Figure 5-2 shows a payment breakdown including mortgage insurance. Keep in mind that your homeowner's association dues are paid directly to your homeowner's association and, therefore, are not counted in the total you would be paying directly to your lender.

Escrow Accounts

When you get a mortgage, you make your payment to the lender every

Breakdown Of A Monthly Mortgage Payment (PITI) With MI		
Principal		$137
Interest	+	$1,234
Taxes	+	$229
Mortgage Insurance	+	$98
Insurance	+	$87
Monthly Payment	=	**$1,785**

Figure 5-2

month. Most lenders are going to require that you establish an escrow account with them to manage the payment of your property taxes and property insurance (your T and I portions). An escrow account is an account managed by the lender to which the T and I parts of your mortgage payment is made; the money in this account will be used to pay your property taxes and property (hazard) insurance when those bills come due. (This is different from an escrow service, which I will explain in Chapter 8).

In some instances you, as the homeowner, can manage your own escrow by saving your money and paying the tax bill when it is due. Your mortgage professional will go into more detail on this since the reason for choosing not to escrow will vary by lender. In addition, some lenders charge a higher interest rate if you choose not to escrow your taxes and insurance. However, most lenders do require the escrow account, and most homeowners like it because they do not have to worry about saving for and making those payments on their own. It works to your advantage also because when you write your check every month, you are done with it; thus, you won't be tempted to use the extra money that is really supposed to be paid towards your taxes or insurance.

Mortgage Insurance
If you are obtaining a loan and are putting less than 20% down, you will be required to pay mortgage insurance, sometimes known as MI (also known as private mortgage insurance or PMI.) The insurance is designed to reimburse the lender for a percentage of the loan in the event you stop making payments and default on the loan. When you sit down with a mortgage professional, you will be able to calculate the cost of mortgage insurance, if applicable. MI is collected monthly as part of your mortgage payment.

You do not have to pay MI for the entire life of your loan. Once you have reached 78% loan-to-value on your home, MI falls off automatically. But don't rely on your lender to keep track of your home value. However, you will have a rough idea of what your home is worth over time, so at the point you feel your loan balance is 80% of the value, contact your lender to find out their procedure to have the mortgage insurance removed. You will more than likely have to furnish the lender with an independent appraisal to prove to them the value of your home.

Since I am talking about loan-to-value, let me describe what that is. Loan-to-value (LTV) is your loan balance divided by the value of your home. For example, if you owed $140,000 to the lender and your home was worth $155,000, your LTV would be 90%.

With an FHA loan (which I will describe in the pages ahead), there not only is a monthly mortgage insurance premium, but also an upfront premium. As of this writing, the current upfront premium with FHA loans is 1.75% of the loan amount. The plus side, however, with the FHA upfront fee is that the amount can be built into the loan so you don't have to have that money in addition to your down payment and closing costs.

One bonus the U.S. Government offers you is that the upfront MI paid is tax-deductible. You will want to check with your CPA or tax preparer, but as of this writing, you can deduct 1/7th of the upfront MI paid per year. (You would take the amount of upfront MI paid and divide it by seven years).

Homeowner's Association (HOA) Dues

If you are buying a condo-type home, your homeowner's insurance will be paid by the HOA as part of your HOA dues. The HOA maintains insurance on the structure of your building, and you in turn obtain a renter's insurance-type (content / H0-6) policy to cover the contents within your unit. This payment is something to bear in mind when you are figuring out how much you can afford. Not all homes or neighborhoods will have a HOA, so check with your real estate agent for details.

When comparing loan programs and lenders, you want to consider only the payment calculations of the Principal and Interest. Your taxes, insurance, and HOA dues, if applicable, will remain fixed regardless of your loan program. So, the only way to determine the actual cost of the money you are borrowing is to compare the monthly principal and interest payment.

Figuring Out How Much You Can Afford

Lenders use calculations known as debt ratios or debt-to-income ratios to determine how much you can afford to pay every month for a home payment (the PITI). Debt ratios are calculated by dividing your monthly debt by your gross monthly income (before tax). Usually, lenders allow you to spend up to 28% of your gross monthly income for housing debt and up to 36% for all of your monthly debt including car payments, credit card payments, etc. The ratios can change slightly based on the lender, the type of loan, and your financial assets. Your housing debt is made up of your PITI plus MI or HOA dues if applicable.

In the next few pages I am going to show you how to pre-qualify yourself. However, you first must learn about the various aspects of your financial life; to run your calculations, you must understand the numbers with which you are working. Before we get to the worksheet, let me define the components a lender uses to calculate your debt-to-income ratio. These components are:

- gross monthly income
- revolving debt
- installment debt
- housing debt ratio
- total debt ratio

Gross monthly income is the amount of money you earn before income taxes, insurance premiums, and certain investment contributions are deducted; it is not your take-home pay. A lender will look for a two-year history of this income along with consistent employment. Income from part-time employment or miscellaneous income is typically not considered; however, if there is a history of this income, a lender will consider it.

Revolving debt includes accounts in which the balance changes each month along with the minimum monthly payment that is required. Revolving means that the balance does not have a specific period in which it must be paid. An example of revolving debt would be credit card debt.

Installment debt is debt that must be repaid within a fixed period of time. When you take out a debt, you agree to pay it back by a certain date. Examples of installment debt are car loans, student loans, and personal bank loans that all have specific dates by which they have to be paid back.

Housing debt ratio determines the percentage of gross monthly income you have available to spend for your housing payment (PITI) plus MI and HOA if applicable. This ratio would be the 28 of a 28/36 ratio in *Figure 5-3*.

Total debt ratio determines the percentage of gross monthly income that can be applied to all monthly debts, including housing. This amount includes car payments, credit card payments, and any other debt that has more than ten payments left. This ratio would be the 36 of the 28/36.

Figure 5-3 illustrates current debt-to-income ratios according to lender type.

Debt-to-Income Ratios – 2009 Figures (subject to change)	
Conforming Loan Limits	**FHA / VA Loan Limits**
28 / 36	31 / 43
28% for housing	31% for housing
36% for total debt	43% for total debt

Figure 5-3

Types of Loans

Here is a summary of various loan types. I will talk in more detail about loan programs in Chapter 7. However, for the purposes of pre-qualifying yourself, you must have a basic understanding of loan types.

Conforming Loans

A conforming loan is one that meets guidelines established by the two primary buyers of mortgages in the United States, Fannie Mae and Freddie Mac, both of which made headlines in 2008. Conforming lenders adhere to these guidelines as the loans they complete are sold into the open market to which they must conform. Usually, a borrower must have very good credit to qualify for a conforming loan.

Government backed loans

There are two types of federal government backed loans: FHA loans and VA loans. These loans are not issued by our federal government, but insured by them to reimburse the lender if you stop making payments and default on the loan.

An FHA loan is one that is insured by the FHA (Federal Housing Authority). The FHA is not the lender; it merely insures the loans made by a lender. If you default on your loan, the FHA would have to reimburse the lender for a percentage of the loan. The FHA has programs to accommodate people with less-than-perfect credit, limited credit history, and limited funds available for a down payment.

VA loans are similar to FHA loans in that the VA (U.S. Department of Veterans Affairs) insures the loan, but the VA has different underwriting guidelines. To qualify for a VA loan, a borrower must be serving or have served in the Armed Forces, Reserves, or National Guard and must have received a VA eligibility certificate. A spouse of a service member who was killed in the line of duty is also eligible.

Sub-Prime Loans

A sub-prime loan is one that no longer exists, but I wanted to make you aware of it as I'm sure you may have heard about this type of loan in the news. This type of loan was available to those who had very poor credit and allowed people to qualify for the purchase of a home using up to 55% of their income to qualify. Although Wall Street created and bought these loans, they found themselves in trouble in 2007 when the real estate market began to decline and these borrowers started to default on their payments. When you do the math, you can see why people had trouble making their payments. Up to 55% of their income could be used for housing and 25-30% for federal taxes. That left only 15-20% to spend on groceries, clothing, and other personal/household needs. It would have been just a matter of time before these loans went bad . . . and they did, in a disastrous way.

Now that I've explained conforming and government-backed loans, let's take some time to estimate how much you can afford to spend on a monthly basis using either loan.

Do-It-Yourself Debt Ratio Calculations

Figure 5-4 contains an example for you to review prior to calculating your own debt ratio. In this figure, we are looking at a dual-income household that has credit card and auto expenses.

In *Figure 5-4*, this homebuyer has $1,060 available to spend for a conforming loan while having $1,452 for an FHA/VA loan. In *Figure 5-8* a few pages ahead, you will see that when obtaining a conforming loan, this borrower who has $1,060 available for housing could spend roughly $150,000 to $180,000 for a mortgage loan based on a 6% interest rate. Other factors will determine what you can actually afford, such as mortgage insurance (if you are putting less than 20% down). Keep in mind that the numbers shown in *Figure 5-4* are just examples. The purpose of this exercise is simply to give you an approximation. Since I am unable to estimate what your property taxes and insurance (T&I) might be, I am not factoring those into our housing debt ratio; instead, I am providing a range of the loan amount you can afford. The pre-approval process with a mortgage professional will determine what you can afford almost to the penny.

Had the two borrowers in the previous example had zero credit card debt, they would have been able to increase their amount for housing by $243 per month, allowing them to purchase a $180,000 to $200,000 home. I share this with you so you can see how credit card debt can affect how

Sample Debt Ratio Housing Affordability Calculations				
		Conforming		**FHA / VA**
Borrower's Monthly Gross Income		$3,100		$3,100
Co-Borrower's Gross Monthly Income	+	$2,500	+	$2,500
Total Gross Monthly Income	=	$5,600	=	$5,600
Monthly Installment & Revolving Debt				
Car payment		$389		$389
Car payment co-borrower	+	$324	+	$324
Credit card debt	+	$154	+	$154
Credit card debt co-borrower	+	$89	+	$89
(A) Total installment and revolving debt	=	$956	=	$956
Housing Debt Ratio Calculation				
Gross monthly income		$5,600		$5,600
Housing ratio percentage	x	28%	x	31%
(X) Allowable monthly housing expense	=	$1,568	=	$1,736
Total Debt Ratio Calculation				
Gross monthly income		$5,600		$5,600
Total debt percentage	x	36%	x	43%
(B) Allowable monthly total debt	=	$2,016	=	$2,408
Available Housing Income Calculation				
Allowable monthly total debt (B)		$2,016		$2,408
Total Installment and revolving debt (A)	–	$956	–	$956
(Y) Available money for housing payment	=	$1,060	=	$1,452

If line X is lower than line Y, then line X is what you can spend for housing.
If line Y is lower than line X, then line Y is what you can spend for housing.

In a conforming loan, this borrower can afford $1,060 per month for PITI
In a FHA/VA loan, this borrower can afford $1,452 per month for PITI

Figure 5-4

much home you can afford to buy. I'm not saying that you should take your savings and pay off your credit card debt; doing this would only prevent you from buying a home for another year while you save again. Before making any decisions, the first step in your course of action should be to sit down with a mortgage professional who can advise you on the best way to proceed given your current financial situation.

Let's look at this example in *Figure 5-4* a bit more closely to see how buying too much home can be a problem. As I have said and will continue to say in this book, don't buy too much home for your current financial situation. If you are on a path of rapid growth in your career and your income is rising significantly year after year, you could probably afford to buy a little bit more home than what you would have been accustomed to paying previously in rent. But as I've stated before, don't commit to a payment that could prove difficult for you.

In *Figure 5-5*, I will calculate how much a couple can afford using a much simpler, yet not as accurate, method.

Initially, $2,085 sounds like a lot of money to have left over every month for living expenses. However, unexpected expenses or impulse purchases can come into the picture. I have seen people buy their new home and soon rack up $15,000 plus in credit card debt from impulse purchasing buying new furniture, and then suddenly, for whatever reason, they have to get a new car, thus adding more expense.

After factoring in the payment on a $15,000 credit card balance, there is now only $1,685 left to cover the general living expenses such as fuel, food, entertainment, gym memberships, children's expenses, auto insurance, utilities, etc. But keep in mind, to get the credit card debt paid down, you will have to make larger payments, which will further curb your cash flow. As you know, life can reduce your cash flow pretty quickly. So don't put yourself in a situation in which you will end up strapped. Be very conservative in your estimates.

Buying Too Much Home Cash Flow Analysis		
Annual income		$75,000
Housing allowance @ 31% (FHA)	–	$23,250
income taxes after tax benefits (25% bracket)*	–	$16,819
Car payment	–	$3,900
401K Contributions	–	$6,000
Left to spend annually	=	$25,031
Monthly cash flow ($25,031 / 12)		$2,085
After charging $15,000 in credit card debt		
Monthly cash flow		$2,085
credit card payment (2% minimum)	–	$300
extra to help pay off credit card debt	–	$100
Cash flow left	=	**$1,685**

*income taxes are ball parked at 25% of taxable income. Actual taxes paid will more than likely be less, but for estimating purposes, this is a simplified method to arrive at your estimated taxes owed.

Figure 5-5

Let's revisit the Sample Debt Ratio Housing Affordability Calculations by viewing a second example in *Figure 5-6* in which the homebuyer has a single income and a car payment. My point with this example in Figure 5-6 is that since the borrower has less debt, they can only spend what the Housing Debt Ratio (Line X) allows for.

Use the blank worksheet in *Figure 5-7* to work up some rough numbers on your own. When you have completed it, refer to Figure 5-8 to determine the estimated loan amount you can afford.

Loan Amount Calculator
Use the chart in *Figure 5-8* to match up the payment for which you qualified yourself to a loan amount. You can get an estimate on how much home you can afford to buy based on current interest rates. (Take into account that the payment you have calculated does not include an allocation for property taxes, insurance, and/or mortgage insurance. It is only an es-

Sample Debt Ratio Housing Affordability Calculations

	Conforming		FHA / VA
Borrower's Monthly Gross Income	$5,100		$5,100
Co-Borrower's Gross Monthly Income	+ $0	+	$0
Total Gross Monthly Income	= $5,100	=	$5,100
Monthly Installment & Revolving Debt			
Car payment	$389		$389
Car payment co-borrower	+ $0	+	$0
Credit card debt	+ $0	+	$0
Credit card debt co-borrower	+ $0	+	$0
(A) Total installment and revolving debt	= $389	=	$389
Housing Debt Ratio Calculation			
Gross monthly income	$5,100		$5,100
Housing ratio percentage	x 28%	x	31%
(X) Allowable monthly housing expense	= $1,428	=	$1,581
Total Debt Ratio Calculation			
Gross monthly income	$5,100		$5,100
Total debt percentage	x 36%	x	43%
(B) Allowable monthly total debt	= $1,836	=	$2,193
Available Housing Income Calculation			
Allowable monthly total debt (B)	$1,836		$2,193
Total Installment and revolving debt (A)	− $956	−	$956
(Y) Available money for housing payment	= $1,447	=	$1,804

If line X is lower than line Y, then line X is what you can spend for housing.
If line Y is lower than line X, then line Y is what you can spend for housing.

In a conforming loan, this borrower can afford $1,428 per month for PITI
In a FHA/VA loan, this borrower can afford $1,581 per month for PITI

Figure 5-6

Sample Debt Ratio Housing Affordability Calculations

	Conforming	FHA / VA
Borrower's Monthly Gross Income	_____	_____
Co-Borrower's Gross Monthly Income	+ _____	+ _____
Total Gross Monthly Income	= _____	= _____
Monthly Installment & Revolving Debt		
Car payment	_____	_____
Car payment co-borrower	+ _____	+ _____
Credit card debt	+ _____	+ _____
Credit card debt co-borrower	+ _____	+ _____
(A) Total installment and revolving debt	= _____	= _____
Housing Debt Ratio Calculation		
Gross monthly income	_____	_____
Housing ratio percentage	x _____	x _____
(X) Allowable monthly housing expense	= _____	= _____
Total Debt Ratio Calculation		
Gross monthly income	_____	_____
Total debt percentage	x _____	x _____
(B) Allowable monthly total debt	= _____	= _____
Available Housing Income Calculation		
Allowable monthly total debt (B)	_____	_____
Total Installment and revolving debt (A)	– _____	– _____
(Y) Available money for housing payment	= _____	= _____

If line X is lower than line Y, then line X is what you can spend for housing.
If line Y is lower than line X, then line Y is what you can spend for housing.

In a conforming loan, this borrower can afford $1,428 per month for PITI
In a FHA/VA loan, this borrower can afford $1,581 per month for PITI

Refer to *Figure 5-8* to determine an estimated loan amount
You can download this spreadsheet at www.whyownahome.com/info

Figure 5-7

timate of how much you could potentially afford. Remember that the pre-approval process will provide you with more accurate numbers reflecting your specific situation.)

Home Estimator Based On Monthly Payment & Interest Rate					
Mortgage Payment / Rate	5%	6%	7%	8%	9%
$600	$111,769	$100,074	$90,184	$81,770	$74,569
$700	$130,397	$116,754	$105,215	$95,398	$86,997
$800	$149,025	$133,433	$120,246	$109,026	$99,425
$900	$167,653	$150,112	$135,277	$122,655	$111,853
$1,000	$186,281	$166,791	$150,307	$136,283	$124,281
$1,100	$204,910	$183,471	$165,338	$149,911	$136,710
$1,200	$223,538	$200,149	$180,369	$163,540	$149,138
$1,300	$242,166	$216,829	$195,400	$177,168	$161,566
$1,400	$260,794	$233,508	$210,431	$190,796	$173,994
$1,500	$279,422	$250,187	$225,461	$204,425	$186,422
$1,600	$298,051	$266,867	$240,492	$218,054	$198,851
$1,700	$316,679	$283,546	$255,523	$231,682	$211,279
$1,800	$335,306	$300,225	$270,554	$245,310	$223,707
$1,900	$353,935	$316,904	$285,584	$258,939	$236,136
$2,000	$372,563	$333,583	$300,615	$272,567	$248,564
$2,100	$391,191	$350,262	$315,646	$286,195	$260,992
$2,200	$409,819	$366,941	$330,676	$299,823	$273,420

Figure 5-8

Exactly How Much Money Do You Need to Buy a Home?

After you get a rough idea of how much home you can afford to buy, you need to find out how much money you will have to come up with to make the purchase of a home possible. When you purchase a home, you will need additional money for a variety of upfront expenses (costs) and prepaid items.

Down Payment

The biggest concern for most people when buying a home is always: How much money do I have to put down? Different loan programs require different down payments. One hundred percent financing is nearly impossible to find these days; however, loan programs that require as little as 3% to 5% down do exist. Down payment assistance programs combined with state and federal grants are available for first-time homebuyers. A 5% down payment on a $200,000 house would be $10,000. I will talk more about loan programs in Chapter 7 and more about down payment strategies in Chapter 12.

Closing Costs

Closing costs can vary by lender and across the country depending on what is customary, so I am hesitant to say exactly how much you should budget for. Furthermore, Congress has made some changes that are increasing the costs to purchase a home, and more changes are on the horizon, so whatever estimate I provide here could very well be inaccurate.

However, I can tell you that closing costs include fees such as the origination fee, appraisal fee, credit report fee, underwriting fee, title search, title insurance, recording fees, lender fees, your attorney's fees, city/county tax stamps, and others. Most mortgage professionals who care about building long-term relationships with their clients will ensure that the closing costs related to your loan are as low as possible. Most costs are third-party charges. However, the mortgage professional can control his/her own costs, which include a processing fee, origination fee, and credit report. The mortgage company does not have any control over the other parties costs involved in a home purchase.

A Word on "Points"

When talking with other people about buying a home, you may frequently hear the term "points." Points relate to what is known as buying down the interest rate in advance so you can have a lower interest rate and an overall lower monthly payment. Each point is equal to 1% of the borrowed amount and gives you ¼ % less in the interest rate. For example, on an $85,000 mortgage, one point would equal $850. I generally do not recommend buying down the interest rate by paying points as it will take you around five years' worth of payments to recoup the savings. Every mortgage professional should cover points in detail with each prospective homebuyer to see if buying down the rate would make financial sense. Also, if you ever notice a low interest rate advertised, read the fine print carefully because often you will see this rate is available only by paying points. *Figure 5-9* illustrates a Points Loan versus a No Points Loan.

Points Loan vs. No Points Loan	
Loan with No Points	**Loan with Points**
Loan amount $200,000	Loan amount $200,000
Points $0	Points (1 point) $2,000
Interest rate 6.25%	Interest rate 6.00%
Payment $1,231	Payment $1,199
Difference in monthly savings from paying 1 point: $32	
$2000 (cost of points) divided by $32 (monthly savings) = 62.5 months	
Break-even point to recover cost of paying points: 5.21 years	

Figure 5-9

If you think you are going to have this loan longer than 5.21 years, then you can make a case for paying points. But the odds are against you as statistics show you will refinance every 5-7 years. More than likely, you could do something better with the $2,000 you would have paid for points in this example by investing it to earn a rate of return rather than buying down the interest rate. The one instance when paying points makes sense to me and most borrowers is if you are being transferred by your employer and you have money available as part of your relocation package. Considering that clients are not able to pocket the leftover money, I have had clients use this money to buy down the interest rate.

Prepaid Expenses

Depending on the day you close your loan, you will incur certain prepaid expenses. Prepaid expenses would include the daily interest on the loan from the day you close until the end of that month.

For example, when you make a housing payment, the interest paid is always for what accrued during the previous month. So when you make your April 1st mortgage payment, you are paying for interest that accrued in March. If you purchase a home and close on May 15, you would pay interest from the 15th of that month to the end of the month. Your first mortgage payment would not be due until July 1, at which time you would be paying the interest for the month of June.

Property Taxes

You will also be required to front the property tax portion of your escrow account when you purchase a home. However, the one benefit you have here is that property taxes are always paid a year behind. So, actually, when you close on the purchase of your home, the seller will be giving you a credit for property taxes that accumulated under their ownership from when they last paid the tax bill until the day you closed. This credit will typically be more than what the lender is going to require you to have to fund the escrow account, which is why you may sometimes hear that people had to bring less to the table for closing.

Homeowner's Insurance

When you purchase a home that is not in a condominium-type complex, you will be required to pay an entire year's worth of homeowner's insurance upfront. Then, on a monthly basis, you will make payments into your escrow account to cover the cost of your insurance for when the bill comes due the following year. You would have to contact your insurance agent to get a quote. The lender will advise the title or escrow company how much you will need to pay on a monthly basis as part of your PITI to ensure enough will be in the escrow account to meet future bills. However, in April 2009, some lenders began requiring owners to pay for a renter's-type of policy (content / H0-6) insurance for one year in advance if they owned a condominium-type home.

Transfer Taxes

In some cities, counties, and states there will be taxes charged (sometimes known as tax stamps) for the transfer of a home from one person to another. In some municipalities the seller pays the taxes, while in others the buyer pays the taxes. Your mortgage professional and/or real estate agent will advise you on what taxes you will be responsible for, if any.

Where to Find Money for a Down Payment

The obvious places

You can use the money you saved in a checking or savings account for this purpose along with the money you may have put into a certificate of deposit (CD). You don't want to incur any penalties for taking money out of your CDs earlier than the maturity date, so plan ahead when opening CD accounts.

The not-so-obvious places

You can use money from 401(k)/retirement accounts—but be very careful here. It can be expensive to take money out of such accounts not only because of the fees, but also because of the tax consequences. You will want to check with a CPA before pulling money out of this type of account to make sure you minimize or prevent penalties. Having said all this, though, I strongly recommend that you do not use money from retirement accounts for a down payment.

You can also find money in the cash value of life insurance policies. Normally, you can take a loan against such a policy without significant penalty or even no penalty at all, and pay your policy back. Check with your agent on the details of your policy if you have one.

Gifts

You are also able to receive money as a gift from a family member to use for the purchase of a home. The money cannot be a loan, and you will have to have the family member write a letter stating that the money you have received is not a loan. From time to time, I see parents provide money for their children to help buy a home.

If you are purchasing a family member's home, they can gift you equity that is in the home. For example, if they want to give you a gift of 20% of the equity in the home, they can. All they have to do is write a letter stating so. This gift of equity would be your down payment. I see this often when children are buying a parent's or grandparent's home.

Down Payment Help

Assistance programs

You can obtain a grant from the seller of a home in the form of a closing cost credit. Recently, Congress has made some changes to down payment assistance programs, so these types of programs in which the lender allows the seller to provide the buyer with a closing cost credit have been slowly disappearing. Check with your mortgage professional to see if these programs are still available.

Grants

State and federal grant programs are available to help homebuyers with their down payment. These programs vary by state and change regularly. I am not listing all the grants here for every state because, unfortunately, by the time this book is printed, many of the grant programs I would have listed may not be available. However, take a look at the following websites to find grants that might work for you:

- Federal Grants List: www.hud.gov
- State Grants List: Check your state's housing website (i.e., your State department of housing).
- City / Local Grants: Check your local municipality's website or call your county, township, or city/village office.

At the time of this writing, our government was offering up to an $8,000 tax credit to first-time homebuyers (or those who had not owned within the last three years). Encouraging people to buy a home was one way to help stimulate the economy. This tax credit may or may not be available at the time you choose to buy a home, but the mortgage professional you are working with will know what programs, if any, the government has available to help you.

Major Purchases and Buying a New Home

Countless times I have seen people who have gone out and made a major purchase (financed or had credit pulled for a new car, vacations or furniture charged on to a credit card) that caused them a problem when buying a first home or trying to move from one home to a larger home. They could not qualify for the payment because of that big purchase. Had they thought about the future, they would have been able to plan for both the purchase and the move. Unfortunately, I have found that people often do not take into account how large purchases can affect their credit scores and debt-to-income ratios when they're ready to buy a home (more on that in the chapters ahead).

For instance, you might be eyeing a particular car that you would like to buy. Before you do buy it, however, ask yourself: How will this impact my credit and my ability to borrow housing dollars in the near future if I need to? People do not realize the effect that larger purchases have on their ability to borrow money for a home. Car lenders, for example, don't have as stringent qualifying guidelines as housing lenders; always keep that in mind.

Before you plan on buying a home, make sure you read the list in *Figure 5-10* to ensure you keep your credit intact and allow for a smoother approval process. If you plan on buying a home in the near future, keep this list in the back of your mind.

If you fall into a special or dire situation, it is best to mention it to your mortgage professional right away. He or she can help you determine the best way to deal with it so that it does not hurt your credit and prevent you from buying a home.

I have heard numerous stories from sellers of homes in which the closing did not take place because the lender for the borrower pulled out the day or two before closing. The lender has the right to re-pull your credit report prior to sending the loan package to the closing agent at the title or escrow company. The lender wants to make sure you have not done anything to change your credit scores or debt-to-income ratios. If a lender pulls out, chances are that something changed your credit profile. I coach my clients upfront not to do anything to change their credit profile in the hopes that they do not find themselves in a situation in which they're the ones who have their loan terminated, preventing them from buying a home.

Choosing a Mortgage Professional

Now that I've given you a general idea of determining how much you can afford, it's time for you to take the next step and run the numbers by a mortgage professional to help you fine-tune your calculations for a more precise figure of how much home you can afford.

People struggle with the idea of finding a good mortgage professional with whom to work. I can understand why, considering the number of negative experiences people have had with mortgage professionals and all the talk within the media about people getting bad mortgages or bad mortgage advice. However, there's no way around this; to get officially pre-qualified and then ultimately pre-approved, you must find and work with a respected and trusted mortgage professional.

You can find a mortgage professional at three different types of lending companies. The following is an explanation of each type:

Mortgage Broker

A mortgage broker is the middle man between a borrower and a lender. The mortgage broker can represent 40 different lenders, which means the broker will literally have hundreds of different loan programs to offer borrowers. He/she will have the best ability to accommodate unique loan situations, such as bad credit and self-employment, among others. The broker is usually paid by the lender for bringing the borrower to the lender.

The DO's & DON'Ts Before You Get A Mortgage

Always consult your mortgage advisor when in doubt about this list.

- ❖ DO continue making your mortgage or rent payments
- ❖ DO stay current on all existing accounts
- ❖ DO keep working at your current employer
- ❖ DO stay with the same insurance company
- ❖ DO continue living at your current residence
- ❖ DO continue to use your credit as normal
- ❖ DO call your mortgage professional if you have any questions

- ❖ DON'T make a major purchase (car, boat, fur, jewelry, etc.)
- ❖ DON'T apply for new credit (even if it seems you're pre-approved)
- ❖ DON'T open a new credit card account
- ❖ DON'T transfer any balances from one account to another
- ❖ DON'T pay off charge-offs without discussing it first with your mortgage professional
- ❖ DON'T pay off collections without discussing it first with your mortgage professional
- ❖ DON'T buy any furniture – buy it after you close
- ❖ DON'T close any credit card accounts
- ❖ DON'T change bank accounts
- ❖ DON'T max out or overcharge on your credit card accounts
- ❖ DON'T consolidate your debt into one or two credit cards
- ❖ DON'T take out a new loan
- ❖ DON'T start any home improvement projects
- ❖ DON'T finance any elective medical procedure
- ❖ DON'T open a new cell phone account
- ❖ DON'T start a new fitness club membership if they pull your credit

Courtesy of Eric Mitchell, a California based mortgage professional, www.eric-mitchell.com

Figure 5-10

Mortgage Banker

A mortgage banker is like a bank, but they only provide mortgage services. It is a combination of a broker and a bank in that it funds its own loans. Some mortgage bankers may work with other lenders as well to offer loan products which they may not specialize in. (A broker, on the other hand, will work exclusively with various lenders since they do not lend their own money.)

A General Bank

National and local banks also provide mortgage services. Banks are generally conservative and, as a result, limited in the programs they have to offer borrowers. They usually serve borrowers who fit a certain type of profile with respect to their credit and borrowing needs. If you fall outside of those parameters, you will not be able to obtain a loan from that bank. In addition, based on my own experiences in borrowing money, banks characteristically like less risky loan programs and, therefore, may not have a wide range of programs to accommodate the special needs of a borrower.

Let me share with you an example of where a general bank is more conservative. I had a client come to me who was turned down for a mortgage loan by a large national bank where he had his own banking accounts. As it turned out, I was able to get this client a loan from the same bank that turned him down. The reason was that as a mortgage broker / banker, I work with the wholesale division of these banks, which have different underwriting guidelines from the retail division. Because of this, I would always recommend you work with a mortgage broker or mortgage banker so you have a full menu of loan programs available to you.

These three types of lenders will often have relatively similar interest rates. However, mortgage brokers and mortgage bankers may have an ability to provide better interest rates and a more customized approach to your loan than a general bank because of the structure in which they are established to function within the lending industry.

In my opinion, it is very important to sit down with a mortgage professional either in his or her office, your home, or your real estate agent's office. You may come across mortgage professionals who may want to meet at a coffee shop or restaurant to discuss a mortgage. I personally find it unprofessional, not to mention an odd place to discuss a private matter that should be confidential. What is surprising to me is that many prospective borrowers go ahead and meet a mortgage professional in these public environments. If you start a relationship with a mortgage professional who wants to meet in a non-traditional location, then my advice would be to move on and find another professional to work with. I can almost guarantee that this type of mortgage professional will not be advising you on most of what I am writing about in this book.

Get to know the individual with whom you are working. This will probably be the biggest transaction of your life to date, and you should feel comfortable with the professional you have chosen. You want to make sure he/she has your best interests at heart and will be with you for the long haul, helping you with your mortgages over your lifetime. I am always amazed when I see how some people are willing to conduct such complicated financial transactions by phone, almost as if they were ordering a pizza. If you are unable to meet in person but really want to use this particular mortgage professional because he/she was a referral, that mortgage professional should have the ability to conduct virtual meetings with you using WebEx®, GoToMeeting®, or some other similar type of web sharing software. What is amazing about these software programs is that they allow the mortgage professional to share his or her computer screen with you so you can work together on discussing your potential loan options. I have used this technology with existing and prospective clients who were unable to come into my office to share with them everything that I would have covered if we were meeting in person.

"Test" Questions to Find the Right Mortgage Professional[6]

When deciding on which mortgage professional to work with, take time to ask each prospective professional the questions shown ahead. Remember: just because someone is a mortgage professional does not necessarily

---

[6] Test questions were provided by Sue Woodard of Mortgage Market Guide. www.mortgagemarketguide.com.

mean he/she is a good one. So these four questions developed by Sue Woodard of Mortgage Market Guide will help you find a knowledgeable professional to work with. The answers you get from each person you interview may surprise you. If they don't answer correctly, go find another professional who can.

1) What are mortgage interest rates based on?

The only correct answer is: *mortgage-backed securities or mortgage bonds, NOT the 10-year Treasury Note. While the 10-year Treasury Note sometimes trends in the same direction as mortgage bonds, it is not unusual to see them move in completely opposite directions.* DO NOT work with a lender who has his/her eyes on the wrong indicators.

2) What is the next economic report or event that could cause interest rate movement?

Economic reports are released on an almost daily basis by government agencies and other large data reporting firms. This data can and does impact interest rates by moving them higher or lower on that given day. Therefore it's important you are working with a mortgage professional who has access to an up-to-date calendar of weekly economic reports or events which may cause rates to fluctuate. Believe it or not, not all mortgage professionals have access to this information.

3) When the Chairman of the Federal Reserve known as the Fed "changes rates," what does this mean, and what impact does this have on mortgage interest rates?

The answer may surprise you. When the Fed makes a move, they can change a rate called the "Fed Funds Rate" or "Discount Rate." These are both very short-term rates that impact credit cards, home equity credit lines, auto loans and the like. On the day of the Fed move, mortgage rates most often will actually move in the opposite direction as the Fed change. This is due to the dynamics within the financial markets in response to inflation.

4) Do you have access to live, real-time, mortgage bond quotes?

A mortgage professional you are working with should be able to show you in real time on their computer what is going on in the bond market so you can get a feel for how the bond market impacts mortgage rates. If a lender cannot explain how mortgage bonds and interest rates are moving in real-time and warn you in advance of a costly intra-day price change, you are talking with someone who is still reading yesterday's newspaper and is probably not a professional to whom you can entrust your home mortgage financing. Would you work with a stockbroker who is only able to grab yesterday's paper to tell you how a stock traded yesterday, but had no idea what the movement looks like at the present time and what market conditions could cause changes in the near future? No way!

To learn more about finding the best mortgage professional, I am providing you with some additional questions that may be helpful:

How long have you been practicing?

If they have been in the business more than two years, they should have the background and knowledge to help you properly if they answered the first four questions correctly.

Do you have any references?

This could be a tough one as clients of mortgage professionals may be hesitant to talk with you. But it certainly does not hurt to ask.

Do you have any testimonials?

Having written testimonials from clients is a pretty good indicator of the level of service a mortgage professional can provide. These are often better than a verbal or face-to-face reference.

Do you have a flyer outlining your services and the type of long-term service you provide?

A good mortgage professional will write down and promote the type and level of service he/she believes in delivering to a client. They should also have a personal website sharing details about their practice and the services they provide.

Do you have a client information form/questionnaire for me to complete?
This will show you how serious the mortgage professional is. He/she should want to know details about you and your situation to help you identify the right loan product. You can see the questionnaire I use at www.whyownahome.com/info. The more the mortgage professional knows about your short- and long-term financial goals, the better he/she will be able to assist you in developing a mortgage strategy.

Merely determining how much home you can afford to buy and coming up with a down payment are not enough. As you can see from reading this book, you must take the time to find and work with a knowledgeable, trustworthy, and confident mortgage professional who will help you come up with the most suitable mortgage strategy. He/she must also be patient with your questions and eager to educate you on the sometimes convoluted issues regarding homebuying and ownership.

If you don't feel comfortable with a particular person when interviewing him/her, you can always walk away and find someone else. The professional must be able to not only answer the test questions clearly and correctly, but also make you feel at ease during this complicated and life-changing transaction. There should be no sales pressure of any kind.

In Conclusion

I presented a lot of information in this chapter to help you determine how much home you can afford to buy. I just want to remind you that it will be difficult to pinpoint exactly how much you can afford for a home as this chapter was designed to allow you to get a rough idea. Once you find a mortgage professional to work with, you can sit down with him or her and work up some approximate numbers before you move forward with getting pre-approved, which is what I will be discussing in Chapter 7.

CHAPTER 6
Understanding Credit

Credit is such an important part of the homebuying process that I have dedicated an entire chapter to the subject. Your credit score, which is also known as your FICO Score, is the most important determinate of your interest rate and your ability to borrow. Thinking beyond borrowing, you must understand how your credit score impacts your insurance rates and many other factors in your life as well. Maintaining good credit is and should always be of very high importance when considering your present and future financial situations.

What Is a Credit Score?

A credit score is the numerical result of a highly complex mathematical formula used by the big three credit reporting agencies in the United States: *Equifax*, *Experian*, and *TransUnion*. The score is based on how you have managed credit that has been issued to you by a lender. A credit score ranges from 350 to 850; the higher the number, the better. Typically, a score over 740 is now considered to be great credit (as of this writing).

Listed ahead are the various types of credit or public records that are reported to the credit reporting agencies which manage your credit profile.

Payment history and balance on (these items are also referred to as trade lines by lenders and credit reporting agencies):

- Mortgages
- Car loans
- Personal loans
- Credit cards
- Student loans

"Bad marks" on credit reports include those related to:

- Bankruptcy
- Foreclosure
- Tax liens
- Private liens
- Judgments
- Collections

Credit reports do NOT reflect information on the following (unless you don't pay and you receive a judgment or collection):

- Rent
- Cell phones
- Utility bills
- Private loans
- Hospital bills

For example, information reported about a credit card you may have will show your payment history along with your high and low balance on that card, whether you paid the minimum or more than the minimum, etc. If you make any late payments, that information is reported and, as a result, hurts your credit score.

Credit Reporting Agencies

The three credit reporting agencies in the United States are shown below. Any time you obtain credit, the information is reported to one, two, or all three of these agencies. A lender will obtain a credit score from all three of these agencies and use the middle score to qualify you for the loan.

Equifax	Experian	TransUnion
www.equifax.com	www.experian.com	www.transunion.com

Understanding Credit

The formula the reporting agencies use to figure out a score is complex

---

[7] These five factors have been provided by Linda Ferrari, author of *The Big Score: Getting It and Keeping It*. Her website is www.lindaferrari.com.

and proprietary and therefore not publicly known. However, the following is an interpretation compiled by Linda Ferrari of Credit Resource Corporation. It breaks down five factors used in determining your credit score:[7] *Figure 6-1* illustrates this breakdown.

■ 35% of your score is derived from payment history. Pay your bills on time and avoid judgments, collections, and tax liens and you'll be OK. The longer you pay your bills on time, the less your credit score will be affected. If you are late, however, the score takes into consideration how late (i.e., 30, 60, 90 days past the due date), how much was owed, how recently the late payment(s) occurred, and how many there were. A 90-day late payment is not riskier than a 30-day late payment, in and of itself. Recency and frequency count too. A 30-day late payment made just one month ago will affect your score more than a 90-day late payment from five years ago.

■ 30% of your score is derived from balances carried on accounts. The lower your balances are, the better your score will be. Revolving credit card debt is the most significant factor in this area. Scores are significantly reduced if your revolving credit balance is close to or at your credit limit. The scoring model considers you to be "maxed out" when this happens. If you find yourself "maxed out," one of the easiest ways to increase your credit score is to ask the credit card company to increase your credit limit, and if possible, to do it without pulling your credit. Pulling your credit will create a credit inquiry, which we will talk about later. If at all possible, keep your balances below 45% of your available credit limit.

■ 15% of your score is derived from the average length of time you have had credit. The longer the amount of time, the better the score will be. So if at all possible, never close a credit card account; just stop using it if you no longer have a need for it. Being added as an "authorized user" to someone's older credit card account will help a lot also. The card should be at least seven years old to make a decent impact in this area.

■ 10% of the score is derived from the mixture of credit you have on your credit report. To maximize your score in this area, FICO would ideally like to see on your record a mortgage, a car loan, and a few credit cards. The "magic" number of credit cards to have is three, but it is never a good idea to close credit cards to get down to that number. Closing cards does more damage than good, even more so than having a lot of cards.

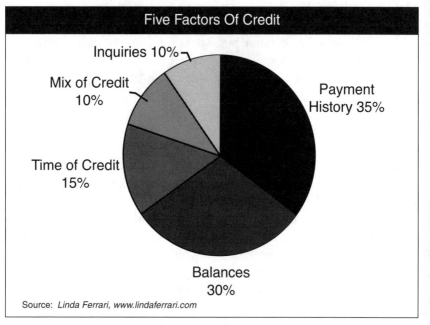

Figure 6-1

■ And finally, 10% of your score is derived from the number of times you apply for credit because each time you do so, you generate a credit inquiry, which can work against you. The number of your accounts that are new is also an important factor. Inquiries remain on your credit report for two years, although FICO scores only consider inquiries from the last 12 months. Important to note is that all mortgage inquiries made within a 45-day period are treated as one credit inquiry no matter how many times your credit is pulled for that purpose.

Your Credit and Obtaining a Mortgage Loan

Once you have made the decision to get pre-approved, and after it has been determined that you have enough income to qualify to purchase a home, one of the first things your mortgage professional will do is obtain a copy of your credit report from all three credit reporting agencies. Any discussions about loan programs, how much you can afford, etc. will be irrelevant until your credit has been viewed. To obtain your report, you will provide your full name, address, and Social Security number. If you are married, a joint report will be pulled. If you are single or buying with a friend or partner, an individual report will be pulled for each of you.

Loans can be made for people who have a variety of credit scenarios. If you have bad or limited credit, a loan can be made in many cases, but the loan process will be a bit more challenging and you will have a higher interest rate. If you have great credit, the loan process will be a bit easier, and you will get a competitive interest rate along with access to all loan programs. Regardless of your credit situation, once you own a home, the process will have been well worth it as having a mortgage on your credit report will improve your credit score over time.

Obtaining a Copy of Your Credit Report

You can obtain a free copy of your credit report at www.annualcreditreport.com, which is a central website to access your report from each of the three credit reporting agencies. The U.S. Government mandates that you are entitled to receive a free copy once per year of your report from each of the three credit reporting agencies. From this central website, you can view all three at the same time, or you can space it out over a year by looking at one every four months. This free report will not give you your credit scores. However, the reporting agencies do offer you the option to purchase your score for $6 to $8 per score as an upgrade when you are ordering your free report. The report you are entitled to receive from this service does not count as an inquiry on your credit.

Note that this free version of your credit report is for informational purposes only and cannot be used to obtain credit. Only a credit report pulled by a lender can be used to determine your credit status. If you plan to buy in the next year, I suggest you sit down with a mortgage professional prior to getting pre-approved and have him or her pull a copy of your report for a fee (usually less than $25). This report will provide you with a more accurate accounting of how a lender is going to view your credit. Should there be anything on the report that requires fixing, you can work with your mortgage professional to get those issues rectified.

Fixing Errors on Your Report

From time to time, an unexpected error can be reported on your credit report. This could result from a situation in which someone has a similar name or Social Security number (which got mixed up on an application for credit). If you are pulling a copy on your own, each of the three credit reporting agencies will provide online methods to dispute the errors so you can get them corrected. You can also visit the library or a bookstore to read up on repairing credit report errors.

In addition, you can use the services of a credit repair and education firm to help you correct errors or reestablish your credit. You can ask for a referral from the mortgage professional you are working with.

When you are in the process of obtaining a mortgage loan, the mortgage professional can assist you in fixing errors through what is known as "rapid rescore." This is a service in which a mortgage professional can provide the agency they used to pull credit reports with documentation you have proving that the information in question is an error. Within 48 hours, a credit score can be improved.

For example, the report I had for a client who was purchasing a home expired, and I had to pull a new one prior to closing. To my amazement, her credit score had dropped 85 points from our initial report, thus disqualifying her from the loan program we had chosen and for which we had gotten approved. In looking at this report more closely, I noticed a 60-day late payment on a credit card. I contacted the client, who said the card had been paid off two months earlier. Upon calling the credit card company, she found out that the last payment had been made, but the way the credit issuer was calculating interest resulted in an $8.53 balance that still needed to be paid. She never received any further statements from the credit card company because, for whatever reason, a statement was returned to the credit card company as undeliverable. The company never contacted her by phone to advise her of anything wrong. She assumed this card had been paid off, but that was not so. Had we not re-pulled the credit report, this could have turned into a 120-days' late payment, and the issue would have been turned over to a collection agency, creating a huge mess to clean up.

Fortunately, the client was able to get the issue resolved with the credit card company, who then issued a letter stating the error and the fact that it would be corrected. I was then able to take this letter and provide it to the company I used to pull credit reports to have a "rapid rescore" completed. The client's score went back to where it was before, and we were able to close the loan on time. Imagine the stress my client endured when she thought there could be a possibility of being unable to buy the home due to an $8.53 error!

From this story, you can see that when paying off a credit card bill that has not been paid off in a while, you should call your credit card company to find out the final payoff amount. Once you pay the final bill, you can also call or go online to make sure the balance on your account is zero. Additionally, it's a good idea to subscribe to a credit monitoring service to advise you of any negative changes to your credit report.

What if You Don't Have Much Credit?

Some first-time homebuyers may not have yet established a lot of credit that would be reported on a credit report. They may not have obtained a car loan, or may not even hold a credit card. Thus, there will not be enough credit history on the credit report for a lender to make an adequate decision. Consequently, some lenders will allow for alternative forms of credit such as rent, utility bills, and cell phone bills, among others. These types of credit do not show up on your credit report. If you can provide proof of those payments (cashed checks, statement from landlord, etc.), it will help you get approved for a home loan.

The ideal situation would be to have at least one trade line, such as a credit card or car payment, documented on your credit report for a minimum of one year. However, you ultimately want to have three to five trade lines on your credit report as you get older.

Examples could be:

- 3 credit cards and 1 car payment
- 2 credit cards, 1 car payment, 1 installment loan
- 2 credit cards, 1 student loan, 1 installment loan

What if You Have Bad Credit?

At the time of this writing, the minimum credit score most lenders would allow was 620. It was only a short time ago that the minimum score was in the low 500s. Although FHA loans don't require a credit score, the vast majority of lenders who provide FHA loans have the 620 minimum score as a requirement.

This book was written for those who have maintained good credit and therefore have the minimum score necessary to become approved. If your scores are low, you just may need a little time on your side to manage your finances better. Credit reporting agencies as you have read prefer a balance of credit and a history of positive financial management. Be patient as it may take you some time to improve your scores into a range that is acceptable by lenders. As I have previously stated, lenders prefer a 620 or better score right now. This number can change as it has changed rather frequently over the last year as lenders became stricter with their lending decisions.

To learn more about improving your credit, you can obtain books from the library or order a copy of Linda Ferrari's book, *The Big Score: Getting It and Keeping It*, available at www.lindaferrari.com.

CHAPTER 7

Getting Pre-Approved to Buy a Home

Getting pre-approved is the formal process of finding out if a lender will allow you to borrow money to buy a home. After getting some idea as to how much home you can afford from pre-qualifying, the next step is to complete a loan application with a mortgage professional and get pre-approved. By doing so, you can then begin shopping for your new home. The pre-approval will provide you with the maximum amount of money you can afford to borrow.

The biggest problem (and a huge embarrassment for many) in the homebuying process is that prospective buyers go looking for homes without even knowing how much they can afford. Some real estate agents will show people homes without knowing if they have been pre-approved. The situation you want to avoid is finding a home you like but soon learning there is no way that you can afford that home, leading you back to square one. Not only will your time be wasted, the real estate agent's time will be wasted as well, and you will more than likely be too embarrassed to go back to that real estate agent.

Do it the right way and get pre-approved before looking at homes. When you get pre-approved, you will be issued a letter/certificate that you can show the real estate agent. He/she will also take you more seriously at this point and do a much better job for you. You will then be able to make the best use of your time by looking only at homes you can afford to buy.

The pre-approval process involves six steps when working with a mortgage professional:

1. Determining your creditworthiness by checking your credit.
2. Discussion of loan programs relevant to your borrowing situation.
3. Completing a loan application.
4. Verifying your income / employment / deposits.

5. Processing your loan application using an automated underwriting system that can provide a preliminary approval.
6. Issuance of a pre-approval letter.

Determining Creditworthiness

As part of the pre-approval process, the mortgage professional you have chosen to work with is going to want to learn about your creditworthiness. Unfortunately, this process can feel somewhat intrusive, as this level of inquiry does not exist for obtaining a car loan or most other types of applications for credit. However, you must be prepared to discuss your finances in detail with the mortgage professional. I will point out that you should not be embarrassed if you have credit blemishes or you don't think you are where you should be financially. The mortgage professional does not care and will not pass any judgment or criticize. All the mortgage professional wants to understand is the big picture so that he/she can do the best job in helping you buy a home. Therefore, it is very important for you to share the particulars of your financial life with the mortgage professional, without feeling embarrassed.

The primary factors in getting approval for a loan are:

- Income / Job history
- Credit history / Credit score
- Assets

Income and Job History

You must first show that you are employed and have steady income that will allow you to make your proposed monthly mortgage payment.

Two years of employment history is typically required; however, I have seen loans approved for people who have had less than one year of employment history. In addition, the underwriter at the lender will look closely at the form of income. For example, a commission-only salesperson will have a difficult time getting approved unless there are two years or more of a solid work and income history.

Different loan programs exist for people with different types of income. Your mortgage professional will be able to help you find a lender that can work with your particular situation.

Typical incomes that lenders consider are:

- Salary
- Hourly wage (provided hours worked are consistent)
- Bonuses (if there is a history)
- Commission (if there is a history)
- Overtime (if there is a history)
- Self Employment

Other sources of income that can be considered for qualifying—provided there is a history and documentation proving this income will continue—are:

- Part-time income
- Retirement income
- Social Security income
- Disability income
- Alimony and child support payments received
- Interest and dividend income
- Rental income from other real estate owned

If You Are Self-Employed

Obtaining a loan is not always simple for self-employed people because they typically use many deductions on their income taxes and, therefore, do not show enough income to qualify. At the time of this writing, many loan programs designed to help self-employed people purchase and refinance homes had disappeared. Times have changed; the documentation of income has never been more important. In addition, keep in mind that if you are self-employed, you will need a two-year history of self-employment.

As a self-employed person, you want to maintain pristine credit and document a reasonable amount of income to qualify for the purchase or refinance of a home. You should review your situation with a mortgage professional to learn about current loan programs that can help you.

If you know you might be buying a home in the next couple of years, you may want to cut back a little on deducting some of the extras you may not ordinarily deduct on your taxes. As always, please have your CPA / tax preparer advise you on the correct accounting for your situation.

Credit History and Credit Score

As you learned in Chapter 6, your credit history and credit score are very important parts of the homebuying process. The mortgage professional is going to ask you for your Social Security number and pull a copy of your credit report from all three credit reporting agencies. From the credit report, the mortgage professional will be able to determine your credit score and what monthly obligations you have, such as car payments, credit card payments, and student loans.

The credit report will also show if you have ever filed for bankruptcy or experienced foreclosure; it will also show if liens or collections have been placed against you.

The lender will use the middle credit score. For example, if TransUnion shows a 721, Equifax shows a 749, and Experian shows a 734, the lender will use the 734 credit score to qualify you for the new loan.

In Chapter 5, we talked about debt-to-income ratios. If you remember, the ratio for a conforming loan was 28/36. The car payments, credit card payments, and all other monthly obligations will be totaled from the credit report and used to make sure you do not exceed the 36 part of the 28/36 equation when factoring your housing payment (PITI).

Assets

Another factor that determines your creditworthiness is your assets, such as investments, retirement accounts, savings, etc. As a first-time homebuyer, you may not have many assets yet. However, any asset you do have at this point is helpful to the loan process. Ideally, as you grow older, you are doing some investing and saving, eventually increasing your assets, which will make moving up to a larger home or a second home later in life a bit easier. When you have more assets along with a great credit score, the debt ratios will become a bit more flexible as a lender will believe you can afford more. This situation is extremely beneficial when it comes to qualifying for a second home, vacation home, or investment property.

However, the biggest asset with which the lender will be concerned is the amount of money you have for a down payment and its source. They want to make sure the money is yours and not a loan from somebody else. If it is your own money, the lender will want to see it in your banking or investment accounts. If the money was a gift, the lender must see proof that the money was transferred into your checking account as well as a letter of explanation from the person who is giving you the gift stating the money was a gift and not a loan.

The lender looks at the following assets when considering your loan application:

- Earnest money you used with a purchase contract (deposit with real estate contract)
- Checking and savings accounts
- Certificates of deposit
- Retirement accounts / investments
- Equity in other real estate you own
- Equity from your existing home (if you are not a first-time home buyer)
- Gift funds or gift of equity

Although assets are essential, they are not the most important factor a lender considers when determining your ability to borrow funds. Many home loan transactions are completed daily for people who have limited or no assets. Still, having assets gives you more flexibility in terms of how you borrow money when you are obtaining a conforming loan.

Selecting a Loan Program

Many different loan programs are available in the marketplace. Each lender offers a set of programs, which can number 20 or more. With nearly 100 lenders in the marketplace, over 2,000 loan programs are offered now. Many of them are similar, but may have different qualifying requirements because each lender's criteria for approving a loan for you will differ. To make matters more complicated, loan programs vary by state.

To keep this section simple and understandable, I will give you just an overview of the different loan program types. Since every borrower is in different circumstances, you will dig a little deeper into specific programs that are best for you and your borrowing situation only when you sit down with a mortgage professional.

The two primary categories of loan programs are fixed-rate mortgages and adjustable-rate mortgages (with a few variations). Keep in mind that it is almost impossible to decide on the best loan product for you on your own. Because so many variations exist in the market, only a knowledge-able mortgage professional will be able to present you with the various options to best meet your short- and long-term home financing goals.

In any case, let's take a look at the fundamentals so you can have a general understanding before going to a mortgage professional. Keep in mind, the words "mortgage" and "loan" are used interchangeably. I will use the common name for each loan type in the descriptions ahead. Loan program types include:

- Fixed-rate mortgages
- Adjustable-rate mortgages (ARMs)
- Option ARMs
- Interest-only loans

- Balloon loans
- Home equity lines
- Jumbo loans

Fixed-rate mortgages

A fixed-rate mortgage has a fixed interest rate for the life of the loan. Your monthly mortgage payment will be the same every month until the mortgage is paid off. One part of the mortgage payment will go toward payment of the interest while the remaining part will go toward paying down the principal.

> **Terms:** 15, 20, 25, 30, 40, and 50-year fixed-rate mortgages
> **Most Common:** 15 and 30-year fixed-rate mortgages
> **Options:** Interest-only options available
> **Example:** $250,000 loan over 30 years at 7% yields a $1,663 monthly payment. $250,000 loan over 15 years at 7% yields a $2,247 monthly payment

You will see that when the loan is spread out over a 30-year term, you will have a lower monthly payment. Since the payment is what qualifies you for a loan, a "30-year fixed" makes the home more affordable to a first-time homebuyer. Most advertised interest rates are based on a 30-year fixed-rate mortgage. For a term less than 30 years, you can expect your interest rate to be lower; for a term longer than 30 years, you can expect the rate to be higher.

Adjustable-rate mortgages (ARMs)

An adjustable-rate mortgage (often referred to as an ARM) has a fixed-interest rate for a specific period giving you a fixed monthly payment. However, once the fixed period expires, your interest rate will fluctuate; thus, your monthly payments will differ. ARMs typically have lower interest rates than fixed-rate mortgages because you are sharing in the risk with the lender for your loan.

Let's say you get a 30-year fixed-rate loan at 6.5%. Should the market change and interest rates near 8% a few years later, the lender is losing out since you are locked in at 6.5%. However, if you have a 5-year ARM, the lender is going to be able to change the interest rate they are charging you at the end of five years to accommodate for the market change. This is why lenders often price ARMs with rates that are lower than that of a 30-year fixed. But this is not always the case since there are times when a 30-year fixed-rate loan is priced less than an ARM. The current market dictates interest rates and what loan programs have the best rates.

So why would you get an ARM? Loan products are designed to meet certain borrowing situations. Let's say you buy a home and you know up front you will probably be there only 5-6 years. If the interest rate is lower for a 7-Year ARM than a 30-year fixed, you may want to consider the ARM since you are minimizing the cost of the money you are borrowing over time. To translate this to dollars, if the ARM was $42 less per month over six years, you would be saving $3,042 over that period.

Here are the details about Adjustable Rate Mortgages (ARMs):

ARM Types:	2/28 ARM, 3/27 ARM, 5/25 ARM, 7/23 ARM, 10/20 ARM
Risky ARMs:	Option ARMs
Options:	Interest-only option
Term:	30 years

For instance, a 2/28 ARM means your interest rate is fixed for the first two years of the loan and will then adjust for the remaining 28 years based on the margin and index your interest rate is tied to. The loan term is 30 (2 plus 28) years meaning that your loan is spread out (or amortized) over 30 years just like a 30-year fixed.

How Does an ARM Work?
An ARM is made up of:

- An initial rate and payment
- The adjustment period

- The index
- The margin
- Interest rate caps

Initial Rate and Payment

A 5-year ARM is going to have a fixed payment for the first five years. If you obtain a $250,000 mortgage loan at 6.5% interest amortized over 30 years, your payment would be $1,580 per month every month for the first five years.

The Adjustment Period

This is the time between interest rate changes. With the 5-year ARM example, your adjustment period would be five years. Your interest rate could then adjust monthly, quarterly, or annually after that period depending on the terms of the ARM the lender offered when you took out the loan.

The Index

When your initial rate has ended, your interest rate is going to be made up of the index and the margin. The index is the measure of the interest rate that the lender uses to adjust your rate. Lenders use various indexes, which are published in financial newspapers daily. They include:

- Cost of Funds Index (COFI)
- London Interbank Offered Rate (LIBOR)
- One-Year Constant Maturity Treasury (CMT)
- A lender's own cost of funds index

Your mortgage professional will have historical data comparing the various indexes lenders use.

The Margin

The lender adds the margin to the index to determine your interest rate. The margin is known as the profit a lender is allowed to earn for the loan they made to you. The margin can vary depending on your credit score and risk factors. Typically, it remains the same while you have this current mortgage, but the index will change as I previously mentioned.

To calculate your interest rate after your fixed period, you would simply add the margin to the index.

Index	3.5%
+ Margin	3.0%
= Interest Rate	6.5%

Interest Rate Caps

Most ARMS will have an interest rate cap. The cap comes in two variations:

Periodic adjustment cap:	Limits the amount the interest rate can adjust up or down from one adjustment period to the next. Often the lender will make your first adjustment higher, while all subsequent adjustments will occur in smaller increments.
Lifetime cap:	Limits the interest rate over the life of the loan, not to exceed a predetermined rate. By law, all ARMs have a lifetime cap.

This is just a basic explanation. When you take out an ARM, you will receive a booklet from the Federal Reserve Board titled "Consumer Handbook on Adjustable-Rate Mortgages," which your mortgage professional is required to provide when a prospective buyer takes out an ARM.

Risky Loan Type: Option ARMs

Option ARMs are highly risky loans. You have to be a very financially responsible person to make this loan product work for you. This loan rate adjusts every month, and, as a result, so does your payment. It also lets you make different payments: less-than-interest-only, interest-only, or a regular principal/interest payment. When you make the less-than-interest-only payment, the shortfall gets tacked onto your mortgage balance, and the actual amount you owe the lender continues to increase. Unfortunately, this type of loan has caused people many problems because they were talked into it by a less-than-honest mortgage professional who might have received a higher-than-normal compensation for placing folks in it.

For example, if you had a $200,000 loan at 6.5% interest, the principal and interest payment would be $1,264. The interest-only payment would be $1,083. The less-than-interest-only payment option might be $850. The difference between the interest-only payment and the less-than-interest-only gets tacked onto your mortgage balance. So, in this example, your mortgage balance went up by $233 ($1,083 - $850) to $200,233. As long as you keep making the less-than-interest-only payment, your mortgage balance keeps growing and your payment will keep adjusting based on the new higher loan amount.

It's important to note that many people who now face foreclosure chose the Option Arm. They used a mortgage professional who did not have their best interests in mind and, therefore, put them in this program. Because these homeowners had problems managing their money, they made the less-than-interest-only payment because it was the cheapest and ended up with a higher mortgage balance, now owing more for the house than what it was worth. The Option Arm has a very effective place in the portfolio of loan products, but it's not for everyone.

Interest-Only Loans

An interest-only loan is a loan in which you only pay the interest. [Recall from Chapter 5 principal, interest, taxes, insurance (PITI).] Rather than part of your monthly payment being used to reduce your loan balance, you will only make the interest payment and therefore your loan balance will remain the same for the term of the loan. At any time you can pay extra with your monthly payment, which the lender will put toward the reduction of your loan balance.

Interest-only loans are used at times for various reasons and do make sense for some people depending upon their borrowing circumstances and long-term financial plans. With the interest-only payment, you will have a better chance of qualifying for a particular purchase for which your income is not enough to qualify for the principal and interest payment. Recall the example with Brett earlier; I was able to approve him for the purchase of his condo with an interest-only loan because the interest-only loan came with a lower payment, thus allowing him to qualify. *Figure 7-1* illustrates the difference in payment between an interest-only payment and a traditional principal and interest payment.

Interest Only Payment vs. Principal & Interest Payment			
Principal & Interest		Interest Only	
Loan Amount	$200,000	Loan Amount	$200,000
Interest Rate	6.00%	Interest rate	6.5%*
Payment	$1,199	Payment	$1,083
Interest only has smaller payment of: $116			
*Interest-only loans have a higher interest rate			

Figure 7-1

Balloon Loans

A balloon loan is somewhat similar to an ARM in that your payment has a fixed interest rate for a specific period (e.g., a 5-year balloon means the loan is due in 5 years). However, the difference is that after the expiration of the predetermined time period, the remaining balance of a balloon loan is due. So, you either have to come up with the money to pay off the loan or you will be forced to refinance.

> **Balloons:** 3-year balloon, 5-year balloon, 7-year balloon, 10-year balloon
> **Amortization Period:** 30 years, 40 years, and 50 years

As I mentioned earlier, my first home loan was a 5-year balloon. Because it was a balloon loan, this meant that after five years, I would have to refinance my home to get a new mortgage or pay off the mortgage in full from my savings (that I did not have). I did not stay in the home long enough to get to that point, but knowing what I know now, I realize that balloon loans may not be the best type of loan in the marketplace.

To better understand the terms of a balloon loan, let us look at a 3-year balloon. If you had a 3-year balloon, the loan amount would be amortized over 30 or 40 years so you can afford the monthly payment. However, since the interest rate is typically attractive, the lender is only going to allow you to keep the loan for 3 years. You will have to pay off the balloon, which is the remaining 27 years of the loan at the end of the 3-year term, or get a new mortgage.

This type of loan forces you to refinance at the end of three years. A balloon loan will often have lower interest rates than a fixed-rate mortgage or an adjustable-rate mortgage, which is why this type of loan would be attractive. However, the person who would be best served by using a balloon loan has a long employment history, significant financial assets, and great credit.

This is a popular loan program for local banks, but a risky loan for a borrower as one may not be in a position to refinance in three years because of job loss, higher debt, bad credit, or some other issue. However, with an ARM, you can continue making the loan payment beyond the fixed period even though the payment is higher. You are then not forced to have to pay off the house once the fixed period has ended. This is why I suggest staying away from balloon loans.

Home Equity Lines (Loans)

A home equity loan is a second loan that is taken out against your home, although sometimes it can be a buyer's primary home loan. People take out home equity loans to do home improvements, to consolidate some debt, or to have just an open line of credit available to them in the event of emergencies. In addition, some business owners have a home equity loan on their personal residence as a backup if their business needs access to short-term cash.

Another purpose of a home equity line is for borrowers to purchase a home and put less than 20% down (this method is not widely used anymore). For instance, a borrower can obtain a first loan at 80% loan-to-value and then subsequently obtain a second loan for the remaining balance less what they put down. So, if the borrower put 5% down, then the home equity line would be for 15%. The borrower would have two mortgage payments to make every month. The benefit in this scenario is not having to pay mortgage insurance, since this way of configuring the loan works out to a lower payment as opposed to having a single loan with mortgage insurance. Times have changed, however, and mortgage insurance is now tax-deductible—for up to $100,000 income—which makes the single loan scenario more attractive.

Jumbo Loans

A jumbo loan is a loan for an amount greater than the conforming limits. Currently, as of this writing, any loan greater than $417,000 for a home would be considered a jumbo loan. Different parts of the country have adjustments to the conforming limit to compensate for the higher cost of real estate. For example, in the Los Angeles area, the conforming limit is $729,750.

A conforming limit is set by the Federal Housing Finance Agency (FHFA) for Fannie Mae and Freddie Mac, the two biggest buyers of mortgages in the United States. The purpose of FHFA is to set loan limits for Fannie and Freddie, which allow them to carry out their mission of promoting homeownership to lower- and middle-income Americans. All loans that fall within the conforming loan limits qualify for the best interest rates in the marketplace, subject to the loan type and creditworthiness of the borrower. The loan limits are reviewed annually by FHFA and may be adjusted up or down from one year to the next.

Those loans that do not fall under the conforming limit are known as jumbo loans simply because the loan amount is greater than the limit.

Jumbo loans are not loans purchased by Fannie or Freddie and are, therefore, subject to higher interest rates.

Position of a Mortgage

Sometimes you will hear mortgage professionals and others use lingo such as "first mortgage" or "second mortgage." These terms refer to the position of the mortgage in relation to its importance as it has been recorded in the county in which you own a home. As *Figure 7-2* shows, a 30-year fixed-rate mortgage will be in the first position. If you take out a home equity line, that would be known as a second mortgage and therefore would be in the second position behind your first mortgage. Legally, this means that if you end up in foreclosure and your home sells, the lender in the first position will get paid first. If there is any money left over, that will then go to the lender in the second position. In very rare instances, a homeowner's entire mortgage might be a home equity line, in which case this mortgage would be known as a first mortgage and therefore be in the first position.

Position Of The Mortgage	
1st Mortgage **(1st Position)**	**2nd Mortgage** **(2nd position)**
Fixed-Rate Mortgage Adjustable-Rate Mortgage Balloon Mortgage	Home Equity Line

Figure 7-2

Understanding Interest Rates

The concept of interest rates can be difficult to grasp when you don't completely understand how they are derived. However, it is very important for you to understand interest rates so that you can better communicate with the mortgage professional and understand the terminology he or she is discussing.

When you get a home loan from a lender, the lender sells that loan as part of a package known as a security. Securities, now known as mortgage-backed securities (often referred to as mortgage bonds), are traded within the U.S. Bond Market. Lenders price interest rates based on the value of those mortgage-backed securities. Since these securities are traded on the open market, their values change frequently. They change because economic news affects the bond market just like it does the stock market. Examples of economic news reports include: Jobs Reports, Unemployment Rates, New Home Sales, plus more. You may hear on the news that the unemployment rate went up; this news could be good for the bond market while bad for the stock market on that particular day, thus improving interest rates for mortgages. Almost every business day, the news released can affect the value of the bonds, not to mention what takes place in the stock market.

Because the value of the mortgage bonds changes daily and because lenders price their interest rates based on the value of those bonds, interest rates for mortgages change almost daily as well. On days with significant positive or negative news, lenders could change their interest rates multiple times throughout the day. Often times by the time you read about interest rates in a news article, the information is outdated.

To further complicate matters, Fannie Mae and Freddie Mac use what is known as risk-based pricing. For example, rates may be at 5.5%, but because of your loan-to-value ratio and because you live in a certain type of condo and your credit score is only 690, your interest rate may now be 6% as a result of the risk-based pricing. In any case, be careful of what you see advertised. Just keep in mind that, depending on your circumstances for borrowing and the time in which you borrow the money, your interest rate will more than likely not be the same as that of your friends or neighbors. These guidelines do change and vary by lender, so I will not be sharing the details of the risk-based pricing as by the time this book is printed, the guidelines will have changed.

Every so often, you'll hear on the news that "The Fed lowered [or raised] rates today." This phrase is a great source of misunderstanding for many people. These "rates" are not related to mortgage (long-term, i.e., 30-year fixed) rates, even though many people assume that they are. They refer to the overnight lending rates from banks that affect home equity loans, car loans, and credit card loans. This "rate" announced by the FED impacts what is usually referred to as the prime rate.

When this announcement is made—that the Fed lowered rates—it does have an impact on the value of the mortgage bonds, depending on what took place. Some heavy trading in the bond market can cause the value of those bonds to change significantly, forcing mortgage interest rates to go up or down shortly after the Fed makes its announcement.

With that being said, mortgage brokers, mortgage bankers, and banks all offer fairly similar interest rates. Rates will, of course, vary from one lender to the next and one loan program to the next.

I cannot say, "Don't focus on interest rates." However, I will say that the interest rate is just one component of the total loan program. Countless times I have completed loans in which the loan program had a higher rate, but the overall monthly payment was less. Once again, it comes down to the loan program that is most relevant to your circumstances. Just bear in mind that it is more important to focus on finding a reputable mortgage professional than thinking entirely about interest rates. My experience has shown me that those who focus entirely on interest rates often get burned from unexpected extra costs at the closing table. If the terms change at the closing table, you may choose to deal with it just to close rather than pulling out of the purchase. If you work with a respected mortgage professional who addresses the same issues that I discuss in this book, you will more than likely be working with someone who will not only provide you superior advice, but also quote you a very competitive interest rate and closing costs.

History of Interest Rates

As you can see in *Figure 7-3*, interest rates go up and down over time. The data that is tracked is for a 30-year fixed-rate mortgage from 1972 thru first quarter of 2009. Rates are typically relative to the times. Interest rates for the second quarter of 2009 were the lowest they had been in our nation's history. It's doubtful that these low rates will be around for a long time, but one never knows. In recent history, the average rate for a 30-year fixed-rate mortgage has been 9.03%.

Choosing the Right Loan for Your Borrowing Situation

After getting all the necessary information from you, the mortgage professional will have a good understanding of your circumstances for borrowing money during the pre-approval process. He or she will then review this information and discuss some loan programs with you. A competent mortgage professional will take the time to put options into writing and

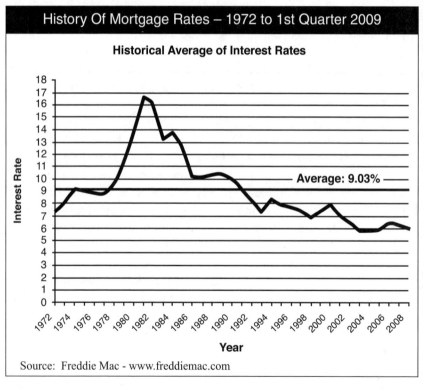

Figure 7-3

discuss the pros and cons of each program. Only at this point will you begin to feel comfortable about the loan program that is going to work best for you and your situation.

Some factors to keep in mind when considering a loan program are:

- Payment (Is it fixed or adjustable?)
- Length of time you plan to live in the home
- Your ability to qualify for the loan amount
- Life changes on the horizon such as marriage, children, job transfer, etc.
- Upfront costs to close the loan
- Down payment amount required
- Income (Do you foresee an increase in your income, or no discernible change?)

When you are ready to get pre-approved, take the time to sit down and talk with a knowledgeable mortgage professional. Request that he or she pull a copy of your credit report so you can see how a lender will view your situation. Remember, when you consult a mortgage professional, you are not committing to anything. If you don't like what you are hearing, seek out a second opinion.

The Loan Application

After you get an estimate of what you can afford and once you have found a mortgage professional to work with, it's time to complete the loan application and get yourself pre-approved to buy.

At this point in the process, you will have gotten past the difficult part in terms of discussing loan programs and sharing your financial situation with a mortgage professional. After your initial meeting with the professional, you can complete the mortgage loan application during the first or second meeting, or via email and fax.

The loan application is just that, an application. It does not commit you to the loan, nor does it commit the mortgage professional to obtain the loan on your behalf. The application also does not commit the lender to issue you a loan. The application is a formality in determining your creditworthiness in the eyes of the lender. In truth, the mortgage professional is generally able to determine whether you will qualify for the loan before the actual completion of the loan application (based on the information you provide and knowledge of various lender requirements). However, sometimes he or she may not be able to make this determination fully until you have finished the application. Certain circumstances, such as poor credit, limited income, job changes, and the like will require a fully completed loan application before the mortgage professional can find a lender who will accept your application.

Once you have found a home, the mortgage professional will submit your loan package to a particular lender who will then underwrite the loan. Remember: just because you were pre-approved, it does not guarantee you a loan until the lender approves your loan application. The pre-approval process is usually a pretty good indicator of whether you can afford a home, but the lender does make the ultimate decision.

The Loan Application – Support Documentation

As part of the loan application, you will need to compile a variety of documents about yourself for the lender to verify that you are who you say you are and that the income and assets you have stated on the loan application exist. To save time and avoid frustration during the loan process, start gathering the following documented information, and keep this information readily available. Furthermore, bring to your loan application appointment copies of any other documents you feel may be necessary.

Documentation to bring includes:

1. Proof of identity: Copies of your driver's license and Social Security card as required by the Patriot Act. (Proof of your identity will allow the lender to comply with the Act, which they are mandated by Congress to follow.)

2. Rental history: If you have been renting, proof of your on-time rental payments will be required for the prior 12 months. If you have been renting in a larger community, the management office should be able to complete a rental history request the mortgage professional will send over. If you have been renting from a small complex, you will more than likely need proof in the form of cancelled checks that your rent has been paid on time.

3. Proof of income:
   a) Copies of your most recent paystub(s) for the last 30 days
   b) Copies of your W-2 Forms or 1099 Statements from the last two years
   c) A list of current and previous employers, their contact information, and the dates of employment for the last two years
   d) If you have a 1099 or a primarily commission-based job, you will need copies of tax returns with schedules from the last two years.
   e) If you are self-employed, you will need tax returns with schedules from the last two years.
   f) If you receive child support payments, alimony, Social Security, or any other income, you will need to provide award letters, statements showing receipt of payments, the divorce decree, or any other documentation, provided you have been receiving these payments and that these payments will continue for the next three years.

4. Proof of assets:
   a) Copies of your statements for the prior month from your: credit union, bank, investment accounts, retirement accounts, money market accounts, or any other accounts proving your financial assets
   b) Additional assets that can be used (but are often not necessary) as proof include a paid-off car, boat, or real estate.

Provide proof of ownership and estimated value of these assets.

c) If the down payment is a cash gift or a gift of equity, bring details of the value of that gift. Your mortgage professional will work with you to draft a letter for the giver of the gift to sign.

5) Proof of creditors:

a) If you are obligated to pay child support or alimony, provide court documents such as award letters, demand letters, the divorce decree, or any other documents showing you are required to make such payments.

b) Your credit cards, car payments, student loans, and installment loans along with the lenders' names will show up on your credit report. If you believe you have other obligations besides those on your report (that you are required to pay monthly), then bring copies of these notes with corresponding payments to be made.

6) Other required documentation:

a) If you are divorced or separated, bring copies of the divorce decree or separation agreement.

b) If you have had a bankruptcy, bring copies of discharge papers from the court.

c) Name and phone number of your insurance agent

d) Name and phone number of association board if you live in a condo or townhouse.

Loan Application Forms

The loan application usually consists of four parts:

1. Uniform Residential Loan Application (Form 1003) (four pages)
2. Good Faith Estimate (one page)
3. Truth-in-Lending Disclosure (one page)
4. Another ten to twenty pages of disclosures that both Federal and State laws require.

Form 1003 – Uniform Residential Loan Application

The 1003 is a standard government form used throughout the United States. It will vary slightly in appearance depending on the software your mortgage professional is using. *Figure 7-4* illustrates the most recent version of the first page of the Uniform Residential Loan Application.

Good Faith Estimate (GFE)

The Good Faith Estimate (GFE), shown in *Figure 7-5*, is another standard government form that is part of the loan application. The GFE summarizes all the closing costs, prepaid insurance, escrow requirements, and your estimated monthly mortgage payment. The form provides an estimate of how much money you will be required to bring to the closing. In some cases, if the transaction is a refinance or 100% financing, you could see money being given to you at closing. By law, the mortgage professional is required to furnish you the GFE within three business days of your loan application. However, most mortgage professionals will provide this at the time of application.

Here is a breakdown of the Good Faith Estimate's sections. (Keep in mind that Sections 800, 1100, and 1200 would be your closing costs, while Section 900 is your prepaid items):

Lender-Related Costs (Section 800)

This section shows all the fees related to the lender and/or mortgage broker/banker including lender fees, credit report fee, appraisal fee, processing fee, flood certification fee, discount fee, origination fee, and tax service fee.

Prepaid Items (Section 900)

This section shows the payments you will be required to make in advance of closing the loan, such as prepaid interest and a mortgage insurance premium.

Reserves Deposited With Lender (Section 1000)

This section shows the prepayments you make to your escrow account, such as property taxes and hazard insurance.

Uniform Residential Loan Application

Uniform Residential Loan Application

This application is designed to be completed by the applicant(s) with the Lender's assistance. Applicants should complete this form as "Borrower" or "Co-Borrower", as applicable. Co-Borrower information must also be provided (and the appropriate box checked) when ☐ the income or assets of a person other than the "Borrower" (including the Borrower's spouse) will be used as a basis for loan qualification or ☐ the income or assets of the Borrower's spouse or other person who has community property rights pursuant to state law will not be used as a basis for loan qualification, but his or her liabilities must be considered because the spouse or other person has community property rights pursuant to applicable law and Borrower resides in a community property state, the security property is located in a community property state, or the Borrower is relying on other property located in a community property state as a basis for repayment of the loan.

If this is an application for joint credit, Borrower and Co-Borrower each agree that we intend to apply for joint credit (sign below):

Borrower	Co-Borrower

I. TYPE OF MORTGAGE AND TERMS OF LOAN

Mortgage Applied for:	☐ VA ☑ Conventional ☐ USDA/Rural Housing Service	☐ Other (explain):		Agency Case Number	Lender Case Number
Amount $	Interest Rate %	No. of Months	Amortization Type:	☑ Fixed Rate ☐ GPM	☐ Other (explain): ☐ ARM (type):

II. PROPERTY INFORMATION AND PURPOSE OF LOAN

Subject Property Address (street, city, state, & ZIP)		No. of Units
Legal Description of Subject Property (attach description if necessary)		Year Built

Purpose of Loan ☑ Purchase ☐ Construction ☐ Refinance ☐ Construction-Permanent	☐ Other (explain):	Property will be: ☑ Primary Residence ☐ Secondary Residence ☐ Investment

Complete this line if construction or construction-permanent loan.

Year Lot Acquired	Original Cost $	Amount Existing Liens $	(a) Present Value of Lot $	(b) Cost of Improvements $	Total (a+b) $

Complete this line if this is a refinance loan.

Year Acquired	Original Cost $	Amount Existing Liens $	Purpose of Refinance	Describe Improvements Cost: $	☐ made ☐ to be made

Title will be held in what Name(s)	Manner in which Title will be held	Estate will be held in: ☑ Fee Simple ☐ Leasehold (show expiration date)
Source of Down Payment, Settlement Charges and/or Subordinate Financing (explain)		

III. BORROWER INFORMATION

Borrower	Co-Borrower
Borrower's Name (include Jr. or Sr. if applicable)	Co-Borrower's Name (include Jr. or Sr. if applicable)

Social Security Number	Home Phone (incl. area code)	DOB (mm/dd/yyyy)	Yrs. School	Social Security Number	Home Phone (incl. area code)	DOB (mm/dd/yyyy)	Yrs. School

☐ Married (includes registered domestic partners) ☐ Unmarried (includes single, divorced, widowed) ☐ Separated	Dependents (not listed by Co-Borrower) No. ___ Ages	☐ Married (includes registered domestic partners) ☐ Unmarried (includes single, divorced, widowed) ☐ Separated	Dependents (not listed by Borrower) No. ___ Ages
Present Address (street, city, state, ZIP/ country) ☐ Own ☐ Rent ___ No. Yrs.		Present Address (street, city, state, ZIP/ country) ☐ Own ☐ Rent ___ No. Yrs.	

/ United States

/ United States

Figure 7-4

Title Insurance (Section 1100)

This section shows a list of all the costs related to the title insurance for your loan. These fees include those for the actual title insurance policy, the title company's charge for using their service to close the loan, notary fees, a preparation fee, an attorney's fee, and a few others.

Government Recording Fees (Section 1200)

This section shows charges related to tax stamps for the state, county, and city in which you are buying. The fees will vary by state, county, and city. In some cases, the seller pays the fees; in other cases, the buyer pays the fees. Yet, in some cases there are fees for both the buyer and the seller. In some cases there are no fees at all.

After all the fees and prepaid items have been listed, this GFE form will reflect the totals and will show you how much money you have to bring to the closing table or how much money you will be getting back at closing.

Truth-in-Lending Disclosure (TIL)

The Truth-in-Lending Disclosure (TIL), as shown in *Figure 7-6*, is a standard government form that allows you to compare the costs of your loan with those of other lenders in the form of an annual percentage rate (APR) (discussed in detail ahead). Assuming you have a 30-year fixed-rate mortgage, this form totals up all the interest you would pay over the life of the loan along with the closing costs and presents the results as an APR. If you are shopping various lenders for interest rates, the APR allows you to compare "apples to apples." Normally, you would want the lowest APR as that would represent the lowest cost for your new loan.

The downside to this disclosure is that it is very complicated to understand. For instance, you may be quoted an interest rate of 6.5%, but the APR might show 7.12%. These two numbers can and do confuse people. Since the TIL is confusing, I find it much easier to pay attention to the interest rate and the closing costs. If you are looking at two lenders and if the loan amount, interest rate, and closing costs are the same, you are being offered the same deal. If any one of those three components changes, then you need to look closely to see what that particular lender is offering.

Let me give you some examples of APR using some uncalculated numbers.

Good Faith Estimate

GOOD FAITH ESTIMATE

Applicants: Application No:
Property Addr: Date Prepared:
Prepared By: Loan Program:

The information provided below reflects estimates of the charges which you are likely to incur at the settlement of your loan. The fees listed are estimates - actual charges may be more or less. Your transaction may not involve a fee for every item listed. The numbers listed beside the estimates generally correspond to the numbered lines contained in the HUD-1 settlement statement which you will be receiving at settlement. The HUD-1 settlement statement will show you the actual cost for items paid at settlement.

* PFC = Prepaid Finance Charge
F = FHA Allowable Closing Cost
POC = Paid Outside of Closing

Total Loan Amount $ Interest Rate: %   Term/Due In: mths

800	ITEMS PAYABLE IN CONNECTION WITH LOAN:	Amount	Paid By	* PFC / F / POC
801	Loan Origination Fee	$		
802	Loan Discount			
803	Appraisal Fee			
804	Credit Report			
805	Lender's Inspection Fee			
808	Mortgage Broker Fee			
809	Tax Related Service Fee			
810	Processing Fee			
811	Underwriting Fee			
812	Wire Transfer Fee			

COMPENSATION TO BROKER (Not Paid Out of Loan Proceeds) :	Amount	PFC
	$	

1100	TITLE CHARGES:	Amount	Paid By	PFC / F / POC
1101	Closing/Escrow Fee:	$		
1105	Document Preparation Fee			
1106	Notary Fees			
1107	Attorney Fees			
1108	Title Insurance:			

1200	GOVERNMENT RECORDING & TRANSFER CHARGES:	Amount	Paid By	PFC / F / POC
1201	Recording Fees:	$		
1202	City/County Tax/Stamps:			
1203	State Tax/Stamps:			

1300	ADDITIONAL SETTLEMENT CHARGES:	Amount	Paid By	PFC / F / POC
1302	Pest Inspection	$		

Estimated Closing Costs

| 900 | MS REQU... BY LE... TO BE... IN ADVA... | ...for | ...at | ...for | mount | By | P... E / POC |

Figure 7-5

Example 1: If your interest rate was 6% and you were paying all your closing costs out of pocket, your APR would be 6% as well. In this case, you have not financed any cost or prepaid item into your loan amount.

Example 2: If your interest rate was 6% and you were financing your upfront mortgage insurance premium into the loan (which you can do on FHA Loans) but paying closing costs out of pocket, your APR would be higher at 6.25%.

Example 3: If you were refinancing your home, your interest rate was 6% and you were financing all your closing costs and prepaids into your new loan, your APR would be even higher at 6.5%. When refinancing, you are able to include all costs and prepaids into your new loan amount rather than paying them out of pocket.

This disclosure provides you with the following:
- Annual Percentage Rate (APR)
- Finance charge
- Amount financed
- Total number of payments and amount paid
- Amount of each payment and due date
- Grace period and late payment charge
- Prepayment penalty notice
- Other details regarding your loan

When you complete a loan application, you will receive a guidebook from the Department of Housing and Urban Development (HUD), which will further explain the Truth-in-Lending Disclosure.

Annual Percentage Rate
The Annual Percentage Rate (APR) is the cost of your loan; it is expressed as an annual rate. This is not the same as the interest rate. The APR takes into account the finance charge amounts related to this loan. Typically, the APR is going to be a higher number than the interest rate you are quoted.

Finance Charge
The finance charge is the dollar amount you will pay for both interest and certain fees.

Truth-In-Lending Disclosure (TIL)

TRUTH-IN-LENDING DISCLOSURE STATEMENT
(THIS IS NEITHER A CONTRACT NOR A COMMITMENT TO LEND)

Applicants: Prepared By:
Property Address:

Application No: Date Prepared:

ANNUAL PERCENTAGE RATE — The cost of your credit as a yearly rate	FINANCE CHARGE — The dollar amount the credit will cost you	AMOUNT FINANCED — The amount of credit provided to you or on your behalf	TOTAL OF PAYMENTS — The amount you will have paid after making all payments as scheduled
%	$	$	$

☐ REQUIRED DEPOSIT: The annual percentage rate does not take into account your required deposit

PAYMENTS: Your payment schedule will be:

No. of Pmts	Amount of Payments **	Payments Due	No. of Pmts	Amount of Payments **	Payments Due	No. of Pmts	Amount of Payments **	Payments Due	No. of Pmts	Amount of Payments **	Payments Due
		Monthly Beginning:			Monthly Beginning:			Monthly Beginning:			Monthly Beginning:

☐ DEMAND FEATURE: This obligation has a demand feature.
☐ VARIABLE RATE FEATURE: This loan contains a variable rate feature. A variable rate disclosure has been provided earlier.

CREDIT LIFE/CREDIT DISABILITY: Credit life insurance and credit disability insurance are not required to obtain credit, and will not be provided unless you sign and agree to pay the additional cost.

Type	Premium	Signature	
Credit Life		I want credit life insurance.	Signature:
Credit Disability		I want credit disability insurance.	Signature:
Credit Life and Disability		I want credit life and disability insurance.	Signature:

INSURANCE: The following insurance is required to obtain credit:
☐ Credit life insurance ☐ Credit disability ☐ Property insurance ☐ Flood insurance
You may obtain the insurance from anyone you want that is acceptable to creditor.
☐ If you purchase ☐ property ☐ flood insurance from creditor you will pay $ for a one year term.
SECURITY: You are giving a security interest in:
☐ The goods or property being purchased ☐ Real property you already own.
FILING FEES: $
LATE CHARGE: If a payment is more than   days late, you will be charged   % of the payment.
PREPAYMENT: If you pay off early, you ☐ may ☐ will not have to pay a penalty.
           ☐ may ☐ will not be entitled to a refund of part of the finance charge.
ASSUMPTION: Someone buying your property
☐ may ☐ may subject to conditions ☐ may not assume the remainder of your loan on the original terms.

Figure 7-6

Amount Financed

Basically, the amount financed is the amount of money being loaned to you—but this amount is actually made up of a few components. The amount financed represents:

- The principal loan amount
- Amounts financed by the lender, but not part of the finance charge such as upfront mortgage insurance.
- Less any prepaid finance charges (Examples include points, service fees, loan fees, credit report fees, and appraisal fees.)

Total of Payments

This might be the most shocking disclosure of all. This disclosure tells you what you will have paid the lender at the end of the loan. It represents the loan amount, plus fees, finance charges, and interest.

Pre-Approval Letter – Now You Are Ready to Shop!

After the application is completed, your credit, income, and assets will be verified. You will then officially qualify to purchase a home. Next, it will be time for you to receive a Pre-Approval Commitment Letter. This letter may be issued the same day that you complete your loan application or a day or two later if your loan application is not fully complete. It shows how much you can afford and allows you to begin shopping for your new home. The real estate agent will want to see this, but do not let him or her keep it. It's ok if he or she wants to make a copy, but you should retain the original.

Now that you have been pre-approved by a mortgage professional, it's time to start shopping for a home. In the next chapter, I will be sharing with you the process of shopping for a home. Happy Shopping!!!

CHAPTER 8
Shopping for Your Home

After you have completed your loan application and have been pre-approved by a mortgage professional, you are ready to start shopping for a home. In addition to having a mortgage professional, you will need a few other professionals along the way to help you complete the homebuying process:

- Real estate agent
- Real estate attorney
- Home inspector
- Radon tester (if applicable)

Working with a Real Estate Agent

The best way to find a home is to use a local real estate agent. Aside from having local market knowledge, real estate agents have exclusive access to information that can be extremely helpful in the purchase of your new home. The best part about having a real estate agent represent you in this process is that it does not cost you a penny.

Let me explain how real estate agents operate. They work on 100% commission. A seller of a property lists their home with a real estate agent (known as a listing) and agrees to pay the agent a commission based on the sale price of the home. A commission for a listing paid by a seller is typically 6% or less. Depending on the market area and the work the real estate agent is going to put into the marketing of a home, the seller and the agent will agree upon a commission. The real estate agent with whom you would be working would share in the commission paid by the seller; therefore, there is no cost to you for the services of an agent who will represent you in the buying process.

As you begin this process, you will find real estate agents who specialize in different areas of their profession. The various agents are:

- Listing agent
- Buyer's agent
- Dual agency

A listing agent is one who has met with a seller of a home and has agreed in writing to represent the seller in the sale of that home for an agreed upon commission. Usually, this would be the agent that has the "For Sale" sign in the front yard and is the main point of contact for other agents to make arrangements to show the home. It is the listing agent's responsibility to carry out the wishes of the seller in the sale of the home. The listing agent will refer all offers to purchase to the seller for denial, counter offer, or approval. This agent will receive roughly 50% of the commission and then split it with the buyer's agent (which I will discuss next). Some listing agents only work on listing homes and might employ another agent on their team to work with buyers.

A buyer's agent is one that represents a buyer of a home. Typically, this agent is not required to have a written agreement, but will verbally agree to research and find homes that meet your criteria. Good buyer's agents will present you with a written agreement anyway to spell out the terms of your working relationship. A buyer's agent will have the buyer's best interests in mind when negotiating a purchase price. This agent will also be able to share local data about the community and town in which you are considering making a purchase. This agent will receive roughly 50% of the commission. You will find buyer's agents who do not list properties but specialize in working with buyers. You will also find buyer's agents who both list homes and work with buyers.

Dual agency occurs when you as a homebuyer are using the seller's agent in the purchase of a home. For example, you meet an agent at an open house for a home that you are interested in. You like the home and want to buy it. You end up using the seller's agent to negotiate and buy the home. The listing agent has to present you with a form to sign that states that, in addition to representing you as the buyer, he/she also represents the seller. If you are comfortable with your negotiating skills, there should be no reason that you would not be able to use the listing agent. However, if you want fair representation, find a buyer's agent to make the offer for you. A dual agent will receive 100% of the commission for the sale of the home.

There are advantages and disadvantages to working with a dual agent, but what remains most important is finding an agent who understands what you are looking for and who will serve your specific needs. I don't see a problem working with any of the various types of agents as long as they provide you with first-class professional service.

Within those broad categories of agents, you will find a variety of part-time agents and full-time agents. You may be best served, however, by having a buyer's agent only when buying your first home. It will make the process a bit easier as you will know this agent will be representing only you and not the seller.

Part-time Real Estate Agents

Many real estate agents work part-time. They may be individuals or stay-at-home parents who want the flexibility that a real estate career provides. Like every type of agent, there will be highly competent part-time agents and ineffective part-time agents. As long as you are flexible in working within his/her schedule, you could have great luck working with a part-time agent.

Full-time Real Estate Agents

A full-time real estate agent is one whose primary income is dependent upon the success of his/her real estate career. Some full-time agents specialize in working with sellers (listings); others specialize in working with buyers. Still, others work with both types of clients.

Some full-time agents have built a rather large practice and have a team of people working under them. In such a case, they essentially become the CEO of their team. Some teams can consist of as many as twelve to fifteen people. This type of real estate group will include a team of buyer's agents, assistants, and coordinators. In the team approach, the main agent is typically the listing agent and uses team members to work with buyers. You may find part-time buyer's agents working within this team environment. Whether you are working with an individual or a team, you just want to make sure your best interests are being served and that you like working with the individual (or team).

To ensure you find the right real estate agent to represent you, use the following questions when getting to know an agent for the first time.

Questions to Ask When Interviewing an Agent

How long have you been a real estate agent?

You want to make sure this agent did not start last week. His/her license from the state will show when he/she first started. You can also look up his/her name in most states online at the department that oversees real estate agents. You want to work with an agent who has a few transactions under his/her belt so that you are best served as a first-time homebuyer.

How many buyer purchases have you completed in the last year?

You want to find out if this agent is successful. You want to see if he/she has good negotiating skills to represent you for the purchase of your home. I would say that twelve or more completed transactions over the last twelve to eighteen months would be enough to qualify as good experience.

What towns do you specialize in?

You want to make sure he/she works in the towns where you want to buy. This knowledge will help you in the buying process as the agent will know the good, the bad, the ins, and the outs of that town.

How will you search for my new home?

You must find out what tools he/she will be using to find homes for you.

What makes you the right agent to represent me?
You want to know his/her skill sets and general competency to assist you. Look for awards, reference letters, education courses in negotiation, etc.

Do you have a Buyer Profile for me to complete?
A good agent will ask you to complete a Buyer Profile. This is a questionnaire that gathers necessary information about your "wants" and "needs" regarding the type of home you want. Agents without a Buyer Profile may not be tuned into exactly the type of home you really want and need.

Most real estate agents are members of the Multiple Listing Service (known as MLS). The MLS is the service that real estate agents use to place the majority of all residential real estate listings. Usually, when agents list a new home for sale, they report this listing to the MLS so that all other real estate agents know the property is available for sale. In addition to having information about whom to contact to view the home, the agent can learn the details about that property including property tax, sale price, number of bedrooms, how long the property has been on the market, and so forth. The consumer-friendly version with limited data from the MLS is available for you to search at www.realtor.com, which is the official website of the National Association of Realtors®.

For real estate agents, another benefit of the MLS is that it provides them with a history of the property you may be interested in purchasing. In addition, it gives comparative sales that you will need to help you determine a price to offer for the home in which you are interested.

Considering that there are so many real estate agents to choose from, the question remains: How do you go about finding an agent to work with? Here are a few places to begin your search:

- **Your mortgage professional can give you a referral**. Often, the mortgage professional has close working relationships with very reliable agents.

- **You can meet agents at open houses**. The agent will be there on a weekend day during an open house, showing the home to prospective buyers (although sometimes the agent may just pay someone to sit at the open house and collect a list of names of people who came through and viewed the home).

- **You can ask your friends or relatives for a referral**. People you know might have had a great experience with a particular agent and would recommend him or her to you.

- **You may know agents from organizations or social clubs to which you belong**. Pull them aside in a professional capacity; explain that you are looking for an agent and want to sit down and talk with them. Use these questions to see if they would serve you well in purchasing your home.

Usually, it's best to choose one agent, provided you are comfortable with that person. You should plan to work with that agent until you find the home you would like to buy. Real estate agents usually specialize in particular geographic areas. You may want to find someone who knows the area in which you are most interested to assist you in your home search. Your choice of an agent will make the difference between having a good experience and having a bad one.

At the start of your working relationship with an agent, ask him/her for a copy of a real estate sales contract so you can review it when you begin the home shopping process. Knowing what it contains prior to actually sitting down with your agent to make an offer will be helpful for you. Otherwise, your head will be spinning when you sit down to make the offer as you are trying to read it for the first time. The print is small and the contract is long, so having it in advance to familiarize yourself with its contents will ultimately reduce your stress level.

Real Estate Attorney
Once you find a home you are interested in and you make an offer that

is accepted, it will be in your best interest to have a real estate attorney review the contract to protect your interests. Many states, including my state of Illinois, require that you have an attorney for the purchase and sale of residential real estate. Regardless of state law, I recommend that you procure the services of an attorney to ensure your interests and needs will be met.

In Illinois, after your offer is accepted, you have five days for an attorney review. (Other states and counties will vary on the number of days, but for the purposes of this book, I will use 5 days. Check with your real estate agent for exact deadlines for your location.) Have an attorney ready prior to making an offer so that when your offer is accepted, you are able to provide him or her with a copy of the sales/purchase contract immediately for review. Furthermore, having an attorney ready will reduce your stress level as searching for one will be one less task you will have to worry about once you have a contract. Friends, family, your mortgage professional, or the real estate agent will be able to help you find a reputable attorney.

The attorney will handle your real estate contract once you and the seller have agreed through your real estate agents on the price and terms of sale. The attorney will review the contract to make sure there are no out-of-the-ordinary clauses or requirements. He/she will also communicate with the seller's attorney to iron out any issues regarding the home inspection.

The Home Inspector

After your offer has been accepted, you have only five days to obtain a home inspection. The purpose of a professional inspection is to identify any areas of the home that might be in disrepair. You will be allowed to be present at the home inspection if you choose to be there. Both your agent and the seller's agent will be there as well.

The home inspector will examine the condition of the home including the structure, the home's systems (plumbing, central air, heat/furnace, appliances, electrical systems, sprinkler systems, etc.), foundation, garage door opener, windows, doors, flooring, etc. A proficient and sharp-eyed home inspector will note everything that is not in perfect condition.

The home inspection is usually completed within a day or two of your having an offer accepted. Because of this time limit, it will be helpful to know in advance whom you want to use for the home inspection and what fees they charge for their services. Real estate agents generally work with a few different inspectors, so yours will be able to provide a few referrals.

Make sure the inspector issues a formal report at the conclusion of the inspection. I have seen both highly detailed inspections with a lengthy formal report at the end and glance-over type inspections with notes scribbled on a legal pad. I'm the type who wants a very detailed report with all issues pointed out, even if they are extremely minor. When contacting inspectors, ask them to send over a copy of what their report looks like along with what their fee is going to be. You will find that reports and fees vary. The highly skilled, detail-oriented type of inspectors will more than likely charge a bit more, but, in my opinion, their examinations are worth the price.

Depending on the size of the home, a home inspection could last one to four hours or more. At the conclusion, the inspector will take you around the home and point out any major findings of which you should be aware.

Once you have the report, you can talk with your agent about the areas that may need to be repaired in the home. You will then communicate this to your attorney, who will then draft a letter to the seller's attorney pointing these issues out and detailing the solution(s) you seek. You may want the items repaired prior to taking possession of the home, or you may want to have the purchase price reduced instead. In some cases, you may ask for money back at closing to cover those repairs on your own. Discussions with your real estate agent and attorney will help you decide how best to proceed.

Your home inspector may find something that requires further inspection by a person who specializes in the specific issue in question. It would then be left to your discretion to seek further information for peace of mind. The home inspector would be able to refer you to a specialist, or you can find one on your own.

It is your (the buyer's) responsibility to pay for the home inspection at the time service is provided, so make sure you bring your checkbook to the home inspection. The fee is roughly 1% of the purchase price, but could vary depending on what is customary in your part of the country. Once again, your real estate agent will advise you on what to expect regarding a home inspector's fee.

Radon Tester

Depending upon where you live in the country, you may have to have a radon test completed. If this is the case, your real estate agent will know whom to call to get the testing completed. Radon is a colorless, odorless, naturally occurring gas produced by the decay of natural radioactive minerals in the ground. Radon can pose very serious health problems as exposure to it can potentially lead to lung cancer. Therefore, this test should not be overlooked if radon is known to be a danger in the area in which you are considering buying a home. A radon ventilation system can be installed in a home to mitigate the radon within the home.

Other Testing

Depending on where you live in our country, there may be further testing or inspections you need to have completed. Some of these inspections may be required by lenders in your area. Your real estate agent and mortgage professional will be able to advise you regarding the requirements for your specific area.

Finding a Home

After you have on hand all of the people you need to assist you throughout this process, it's time to start shopping. As I have already said, you will be best served by using a real estate agent. Before heading out with an agent, you should do some preliminary research online to get a feel for home prices and what types of homes you will be able to afford. The best place to do that is at www.realtor.com.

Realtor.com is a collection of all public listings available in your marketplace. Most of the listings on the website will show photographs and some details about the home, such as room sizes, number of rooms, bathrooms, etc. To narrow down what you are looking for, you can set a variety of search criteria. Realtor.com will not show you details about real estate taxes or homeowner association dues, or other details that may become pertinent in the negotiation process. However, you will get a very useful preview along with some specific statistics on homes.

The version your agent views to find homes for sale is known as the MLS (Multiple Listing Service), which I mentioned previously. Your real estate agent can access this database to find properties and show you those that meet your criteria. The agent will also have access to specific details such as property taxes, HOA dues, how long the property has been on the market, and if the price has been reduced, as well as other important information.

When viewing Realtor.com, print out pages of the homes that interest you and share those with the real estate agent you are working with. This will help point the agent in the right direction so he or she can focus on the types of homes you are looking for while performing their research. The agent can also gather the specific details about the properties you have identified. Once you have some homes picked out to view, the real estate agent will then contact the listing agent to set up appointments for you to view the homes.

Home Types in the Marketplace
Earlier in the book in Chapter 1, I touched on what defines a "home." I will now describe each type of home in more detail:

- Condominium
- Co-op
- Townhouse
- Single-family home
- Duplex
- 3-4 Flat

Condominium

Living in a condominium is somewhat like apartment living in that you are sharing common areas such as the parking area, entry, hallways, pools, fitness center, and the like. When purchasing a condominium, you are purchasing the section of the building in which your unit is located along with, in some instances, a parking space. Some parking spaces are sold separately, while other complexes have general parking maintained by the association.

Every condominium complex has an association that manages the building and grounds for that complex. In most cases, the association consists of a board made up of unit owners. The board makes decisions regarding the maintenance of the complex. In larger complexes, the association will hire an outside management company to deal with issues related to the maintenance of the complex, leaving the board to focus on major issues and long-term planning.

Because each condominium complex has an association, condo owners are required to pay monthly homeowner's association dues (HOA). The amount of the dues varies greatly depending on the building. The association fee is generally for the upkeep of the grounds, ongoing maintenance, and insurance on the building in the event of fire, flood, or catastrophe. In addition, part of the fee goes into a reserve fund so the association has available money to make major repairs or for planned maintenance. Because a portion of your monthly association dues goes toward insurance, you would not be required to obtain your own homeowner's policy. You would just have to get a renter's-type insurance policy (also known as content or HO-6 coverage) to cover the contents of your unit in the event of an unfortunate circumstance or disaster.

If you are considering a condominium, your real estate agent will be able to provide you with the information regarding property taxes, association dues, and any special assessments the condo association is considering. You should ask to see the association's budget and the last few months' worth of minutes for association board meetings. You want to look for major items of repair that will require a special assessment or a big increase in dues.

Some other questions to ask yourself and the association when looking at a condominium are:

- Is the parking secure? (You may want indoor parking.)
- Will I be safe coming and going from the building? Do I want a secure entry?
- Do I need a pool? (Such an amenity is an added expense for the association.)
- Do I need a playground or party room?
- Am I responsible only for the contents contained inside of my unit in the event of building damage?
- Does the association take care of all exterior repairs / replacements?

One other area of concern when considering a condominium would be new construction. If you are buying for the first time, newly constructed condos may not be the best choice. Based on the past experiences of my wife and of acquaintances, I've seen that the association is not yet formed in most newly constructed condos. Things tend to be a bit chaotic until the builder has finally completed and sold all the units—there are issues regarding rules violations, lack of rules, lack of planning, etc. I have also noted that some newly constructed condominiums are overinflated in value because they are new. If you are thinking about a brand new condo, I advise you to be cautious and to discuss this option with your real estate agent.

A big plus when buying a condominium is that you can transition from your rental apartment to ownership without a significant increase in monthly payment. In fact, I have completed transactions for people in which the overall housing payment (principal, interest, taxes, & HOA) for their condo was less than what they were paying in rent. At the same time, I realize that in areas outside of major markets like Chicago, single-family homes are equally as affordable as buying a condo, and your payment could be similar to your rent.

Co-op (housing cooperative)

A co-op is an offshoot of a condominium. Rather than buying a unit in a building as one would in a condominium building, you are buying shares in a corporation that owns the building. Those shares represent the unit you would occupy. With those shares, you would gain the right to vote on matters related to the building such as electing members of the board. A co-op is essentially a corporation that you own stock in for which a lender will lend you money to buy those shares.

The main difference between a co-op and a condominium is that to be able to buy shares in the corporation, you have to submit an application to the co-op board to become approved. This application would include one's personal financial history and personal references. A co-op board can accept or reject your application for whatever reason they choose. The board essentially decides who can buy shares and live in the co-op building and who cannot. In a condominium, on the other hand, you are buying the unit and the board does not nor cannot decide who purchases units in the building.

You will typically find co-ops in New York City and a small handful of cities around the country. You will also find that there are a limited number of lenders who will lend money for co-ops. If this is the type of building you would like to live in, your real estate agent will be able to further assist you in navigating the maze that goes along with buying into a co-op.

Townhouses

A townhouse is set up similarly to a condominium in terms of having an association; therefore, you would want to follow the same guidelines as those for condominiums. The main difference, however, is that with a townhouse you generally have more space (yard, patio, common grounds) and will pay more for the space than you would for a condominium.

The one issue regarding townhouses is the way in which the association is set up. If the association is set up in the condominium-style that I previously described, you do not need to worry about maintaining your own homeowner's insurance policy or dealing with the building's exterior issues. If the association is set up in a way in which each owner has their own homeowner's policy, be careful.

Let me share a story of how I got burned to the tune of $5,000 in this homeowner-style setup. The first home I bought was a townhouse. Each building had six units, all sharing a common roof. Each townhouse was its own home, and each homeowner had to maintain their own homeowner's insurance coverage. The association did not have an umbrella policy that covered the structure, unlike that of a condominium.

The problem for me came into play after I bought my townhome. Hail had damaged the roof of the building prior to my taking possession. The association advised me that I needed to get my insurance company to cover the cost because they were going to have the roof replaced. Naturally, my insurance company would not pay for it since the hail damage took place prior to my ownership. The prior owner's insurance would not pay for it either because they terminated the coverage once I had the home inspection completed. Even after consulting legal counsel, I found myself having to write a $5,000 check to cover my portion of the roof that was being replaced. To this day, I am still bothered by the fact that I had to pay this. However, this mishap has allowed me to share my story with many homebuyers. My experience substantiates the fact that in a townhouse environment (where there are more than two units in the building), buyers need to make sure there is "umbrella coverage," i.e., that the association is set up in such a way that the entire property is insured under one insurance policy.

Keep in mind that in such a case as roof damage, one part of the building might have more damage than the others. But a roofer cannot replace merely part of a roof; they have to replace it entirely. If your unit does not have much damage, your insurance may not pay, but the association is still going to send you a bill for your portion of the roof.

Always make certain your townhouse has a condominium-type policy rather than a traditional homeowner's-type policy. Otherwise, stay away.

If you don't, you will leave yourself open to problems that can end up being quite costly. The only instance in which you will probably not have to worry about the type of coverage is in a "higher-end" townhouse. If you are considering this type of home, then more than likely you have already put money away, you make a better-than-average income, and it may not be a financial burden if you have to pay for certain exterior repairs if necessary.

Single-family Home

A single-family home is a stand-alone residential structure on its own piece of land. Unlike a condominium or townhouse, you are responsible for everything regarding the house and the grounds. For instance, if the roof leaks or the windows break, it is your responsibility to fix them. It's your responsibility to insure the home and to maintain the exterior grounds. In some cases, you may find a single-family home inside a gated or planned community. Often in these developments, you will be paying HOA dues that will cover the cost of mowing the grass, snow removal, maintenance, and other expenses to keep up the community-shared grounds.

Duplex

A duplex looks similar to a single-family home, but the building consists of two units. Each unit owns a portion of the yard. You would have a homeowner's-type insurance policy for your portion of the building. It would be up to you and the person who owns the other side of the building to agree on how the common grounds should be maintained.

Another form of a duplex is a 2-flat in which the units are on top of one another and you might share half the garage and the grounds.

One option is to purchase a duplex (the entire 2-unit building) and rent out the other half so that you have rental income to help cover the cost of your mortgage for the building. If you are open to having a renter and to dealing with landlord/landlady responsibilities, buying a duplex can be a financially wise move.

3-4 Flat

With a 3-4 flat-type of home, you are purchasing an entire building, living in one unit, and renting out the remaining units. With this type of home, you have to be prepared to manage renters, make necessary repairs, etc. Owning a 3-4 flat is a great way to create wealth as the majority of the rent you are bringing in should cover most, if not all, of your mortgage payment.

The challenge you might face with this type of home purchase is qualifying for the mortgage. You may have to count on the income from the rental units to help you qualify. Depending on the lender's requirements, you may not be able to use such income to qualify for the purchase of this home unless you have a history of managing renters. My advice is to find out what the qualifying guidelines are before setting your sights on the purchase of a 3-4 flat.

Additionally, in purchasing a 3-4 flat, you would have to live in one of the units for the loan to be qualified under owner-occupied. If you do not intend to occupy one of the units as your primary residence, then the purchase would be considered an investment and, therefore, different qualifying guidelines and interest rates would apply.

Any building consisting of five units or more would be considered commercial property, so residential lending guidelines would not apply. With this sized building, you would need to work with commercial lenders who specialize in the purchase of a property with five or more units. Commercial lenders include your local bank and lenders who specialize in commercial loans.

What Should You Buy?

Your budget and lifestyle will dictate the type of home you choose to purchase. The best way to get started is to view a variety of homes in your market so you can get a sense firsthand of how property values vary among the different types of homes. You'll find that you will love the first home you look at, but then you may fall in love with the next home you look at as well. My point here is to encourage you to keep an open mind, view many homes, and narrow your search as you find what you like in the price range you are considering.

Once you've narrowed down your choices, do your homework. If you are working with a real estate agent, he/she will have provided you with various details about the homes you looked at, including:

- Property taxes
- Association Dues
- Additional costs of owning that home, such as anticipated utility bills for water, sewer, gas, and electric

If the agent does not know this information, ask and he/she will contact the sellers to find out. You want to know exactly how much it's going to cost you to own this home. You can assume your telephone, cable, and Internet expenses are going to be similar to what you have now if you decide to keep the same services. However, some of your other utility costs could go up from what you are used to as a renter. Also, in a condo or townhouse, basic cable and/or Internet services are sometimes included in the association dues. Be sure to find out what services the association dues include.

When you find a home you really like, take time to consider all its pluses and minuses before making an offer. In some markets, you may have to act quickly if there are more buyers than homes for sale. Still, think about your purchase carefully. You are making a big investment. It is important to make an informed decision so that you will be happy with the home, neighborhood, and community you've chosen to live in.

In addition, take some time to drive around your potentially new neighborhood at different times of the day to see the normal life of the homeowners in relation to one another within the neighborhood. By doing so, you will notice characteristics you might like or might not like about the neighborhood.

Sometimes You Need to Take a Second Look

Before my wife and I bought our current home, we'd hated it the first time we'd seen it. The home was out-of-date and somewhat dirty. The landscaping was overgrown, and the entire house lacked any sort of character. We knew that it would take a lot of time, energy, and money to make it "our home," a special and comfortable place to live in.

After viewing the house, we turned around and saw the same model for sale down the street, which had been nicely updated. The only problem was that the updated house was selling for a significantly higher price. Furthermore, the second home had been updated in a way that was not really to our taste. Replacing kitchen cabinets, flooring, and appliances can get expensive; since this home was updated and, therefore, costlier, it would have been financially unwise to change the upgrades that had already been made. After some thought and conversation, we ended up going back and looking at the first house that we did not like. With much deliberation, we began to see the potential changes we could accomplish to make the house our own. We decided to make an offer on the house, and we purchased it for less than the listing price. Since then, we have transformed our house into a lovely dwelling that reflects the comfort and style of the "dream" home we originally envisioned.

Before we purchased our present home, my wife and I drove around the neighborhood many times at different times of the day to get a sense of the surroundings, and afterwards, we realized we really liked it. We were comfortable with the location and the meticulous ways in which most of the residents maintained their homes. After we moved in and the neighbors saw some of the work we were doing, they came by not only to welcome us to the neighborhood, but also to thank us for making some of the exterior improvements to our house, which had been neglected by the previous owners, creating a bit of an eyesore in the neighborhood.

When you are out looking at homes, keep an open mind. Bring a camera with you to take pictures, and make notes so that you can refresh your memory later when you are reviewing what you saw.

Do You Want the Biggest House on the Block?

When it comes to single-family homes, the biggest house on the block may not necessarily be the best choice. Many real estate agents and appraisers have told me that the big house on the block suffers in value, but improves the values of the other, smaller homes. Don Arceri, an Illinois licensed appraiser, advises to stick to the mid-sized homes if possible when neighborhoods have a variety of home sizes. The smallest home on the block can have the reverse effect in that it can bring values down. You should never have a problem selling a mid-sized home in a neighborhood with some big homes. The bigger ones might take longer to sell.

When considering townhouses in this scenario, end units will always be more desirable than middle units. The end units will sometimes carry a premium price, but to many people that premium price is warranted.

Regarding condominiums, typically the higher the floor or the better the view in the building, the more expensive the unit is. If you're a first-time homebuyer, buying on a higher floor may not be worth it if you are trying to create wealth. The higher payment for the same amount of space may not be justifiable. Check with your real estate agent, who can share recent sale prices of condominiums in a building you are interested in. The agent will be able to tell you whether residences on higher floors sell faster than those on lower floors.

Caution about New Construction

One caution about new construction is over-inflated values for the purchase price. Builders often put a premium on certain lots in neighborhoods or on floors in a condo building that are higher or have better views. If you paid a premium for your home, you may find that a few years down the road when the builder has completed the project, that your home's value may adjust down as people shopping for homes may not feel your home is worth a premium price in relation to other homes in the neighborhood or the building.

Living in Urban versus Suburban Areas

Often the closer you live to a major city, the more expensive housing will be. Regardless of where you choose to live, the same homebuying principles apply. The real estate agent with whom you are working will best be able to help you identify the positives and negatives of the areas in which you are considering buying a home.

Convenience Issues to Consider when Shopping for a Home

When you start shopping for a home, a variety of factors will come into play when you decide where you would like to live. I have put together a list of factors you will want to consider. While the real estate agent you work with will have access to quite a bit of community information, you can do some online research yourself.

- Proximity to schools
- Commute to work / traffic flows
- Houses of worship (churches/temples)
- Shops, especially grocery stores and pharmacies
- Restaurants
- Daycare
- Fitness clubs
- Recreational facilities
- Public transportation
- City / community services

Expense Issues to Consider when Buying a Home

When deciding on a home to purchase, there are expense issues you will want to keep in the back of your mind as well. Different types of homes will have different types of construction that will require money to keep up. At some point in time, something will have to be replaced in your home because it has worn out. As I previously mentioned, a condo or townhouse will require less upkeep than a single family home. Depending on the type of housing you are considering, you will want to budget for potential repairs.

- Yearly maintenance costs – how much money will it cost me to keep up the home such as furnace checkups, mowing the yard, snow removal, window cleaning, etc.

- Type of siding available – vinyl siding will require less upkeep than cedar or brick siding over time. Cedar may have to be re painted while brick might have to be tuck-pointed (repairing the mortar).
- Age of the roof - a roof might have to be replaced after 20 years. Find out how old the roof is and then budget for the fact you might need a new roof in a few years.
- Age of the house's systems (furnace, air conditioner, etc.) - at some point, a furnace or air conditioner will break; find out how old they are and budget accordingly.
- Age of the home – the older the home, the more work in the form of upkeep it may need.
- Condition of the yard - an overgrown yard is going to take more to clean up than a well-maintained yard.

You want to strongly consider all these issues. You also want to find out if you are responsible for repairs and what expenses you could have on the horizon. This will help you negotiate when making an offer and budget once you close on the purchase.

Unique Homebuying Programs

Now, I would like to share with you some information about two programs that could help make the purchase of your first home a bit easier financially. These programs are available to anyone buying a home, but as a first-time homebuyer, you will find them extremely advantageous if you have the patience to go through the process. These two programs are the FHA 203K Rehab Program and the Seller Buy Down Program.

FHA 203K Rehab Program

Many homes for sale have been foreclosed upon and can be quite rundown. The FHA has a program known as the 203K Rehab Program to help buyers purchase these homes and improve them. The best part of the program is that a 203K approved lender will lend you the money to fix up the home to bring it back up-to-date. Generally, these homes are in a bank's possession after the homeowners lost them to foreclosure. These homes are often known as "Real Estate Owned" or "REO," meaning "owned by the bank."

The program works like this: let's say the home is selling for $150,000. It needs roughly $30,000 worth of work to be updated. This work may include fixing the roof; repairing walls or the foundation; or replacing appliances, paint, carpet, etc. Once the home is fixed up, the After Repair Value (ARV) is now estimated to be $210,000. Based on this estimate, you apply for a loan with a 203K approved lender. The 203K approved lender would lend you up to 96.5% of the ARV, which would be $202,650 based on the estimated $210,000 ARV. However, since you only need a loan for $180,000 ($150,000 purchase price plus $30,000 in repairs), you have purchased a $210,000 home for $180,000 and therefore have gained instant equity of $30,000. As an added bonus, you only had to have a 3.5% down payment based off of $180,000 rather than the $210,000.

Therefore, the 203K program can be beneficial if you have the patience to work within its established guidelines. Some of these guidelines include the following:

- The home has to be appraised by a 203K licensed appraiser.
- The work has to be completed by a 203K approved contractor.
- You cannot do any of the work yourself.
- You have to own and occupy the property yourself; there can be no investors.
- The work has to be done within a specified period of time.

In any case, the home you choose must be worth the effort.

The 203K program pertains to homes that require extensive repairs such as those related to the foundation, roofing, siding, concrete, paving, structure, etc. There is a limited version of the 203K program known as the 203K Limited Repair Program, which pertains to homes that need solely cosmetic repairs such as new paint, carpet, and appliances. If you are interested in these programs, consult your mortgage professional or visit portal.hud.gov/ and search for "203K."

Seller Buy Down

The Seller Buy Down program is a loan program offered by lenders designed to make the purchase of a home more affordable for the buyer. In this program, the seller takes a certain amount from the asking price to pay the buyer's lender to buy down the interest rate on the buyer's new mortgage; the seller does this instead of lowering their asking price of the home. In this way, the home is more affordable for the buyer as they will have a lower payment as a result of having a lower interest rate on their new mortgage.

The program is a win-win situation. The seller gets to sell their home more quickly because they have a larger pool of potential buyers; the buyer can now afford the home because of the lower housing payment the buy down provides. With the Seller Buy Down, the real estate agents and the seller need to both understand the use of the Seller Buy Down program before the transaction can be completed.

Figure 8-1 shows an example of how the program works when a seller keeps their selling price at $190,000 rather than lowering it to $180,000. The seller will use the difference of $10,000 to buy down the interest rate for the buyer to make monthly payments more affordable.

Seller Buy Down Program			
No Buy Down		**With Buy Down**	
Purchase price	$180,000	Purchase price	$190,000
Down payment	$9,000	Down payment	$9,000
Loan amount	$171,000	Loan amount	$181,000
Interest rate	6.00%	Interest rate	4.75%
Monthly payment	**$1,025**	**Monthly payment**	**$944**
Monthly savings with reduced payment with Buy Down: $81			
Income to qualify for the lower payment is: $289 less			

Figure 8-1

The popularity and acceptance of this program comes and goes depending on the lender and the type of buying and selling market we are in. For example, in a buyers' market, home sellers are often forced to lower their asking price. So rather than lower the asking price, the seller will pay to lower your interest rate to make the mortgage payment more affordable; in this way, you as the buyer can benefit from this program. In a sellers' market, sellers are not pressured to lower their asking price and therefore the demand for a Seller Buy Down will not be practical as the seller can usually get their full asking price for the home from you, the buyer. The guidelines for these programs change from time to time as a result of the market, so check with your mortgage professional on what is currently being offered by lenders.

Buying through a FSBO (For Sale By Owner)

Some homes for sale are through For Sale By Owners (FSBOs). Most real estate agents will not show you FSBO homes mainly because FSBO (pronounced "Fiz Bow") homes are not listed in the MLS. Prospective buyers discover most FSBO homes by seeing a "For Sale By Owner" sign while driving by a home or by seeing advertisements in the "Homes for Sale" section of the local newspaper.

You may have an agent who is tuned into your area of interest and may contact a FSBO directly to see if they are open to showing their home and to paying a commission to the agent for bringing the buyer to them. Usually, most FSBOs will be open to paying this commission. You can also contact a FSBO directly on your own and work with them to make an offer and to purchase their home without using a real estate agent's services. Just keep in mind that if the agent makes contact with the FSBO first, you may have a legal responsibility to use the services of that agent alone if you want to purchase the home.

Whether you are buying a home that has been listed by a real estate agent or one being sold by a FSBO, the purchase/sale process will be the same.

Making an Offer

Once you have found a home you have an interest in buying, it's time to make an offer with your real estate agent. In short, these steps are:

- You will meet with your agent and write up an offer.
- Your agent will present the offer to the seller's agent or the seller if acting as a dual agent.
- You will add contingencies to the offer (i.e., the purchase is subject to certain conditions).
- You will provide earnest money.
- The seller will counter offer.
- You will counter offer back.
- Eventually you and the seller will agree on a purchase price.
- You will now have a contract for purchase.
- You enter escrow (in some states).

I will describe each of these steps in the next few sections.

Meeting with Your Agent to Make the Offer

When you make an offer, you will sit down with your real estate agent and complete a Real Estate Contract. In some states or counties, you may complete a Binder which has the basic details of the offer, while then completing a formal contract once you have settled on the terms with the seller. The contract name and initial process will vary slightly by state and the local Realtor Board. In Illinois the contract is referred to as a "Residential Real Estate Contract." For the purposes of this book, I will refer to the initial offer as a "contract."

As I mentioned earlier, it would be a good idea to get a copy of the contract up front. Reviewing it in advance will help alleviate some of the stress on the day you are putting together the offer with your agent. It's best to have a solid understanding ahead of time of the document you will be signing so there are no surprises.

The contract is a legal agreement between you and the seller. The contract will include extensive information regarding personal details such as your name, your address, etc., but will also include the purchase price you are willing to pay along with certain terms, such as your desired closing date or the repairs you want the seller to make. These terms are known as contingencies.

The contract will also include any items you want included with the purchase, such as the fridge, oven, or microwave. Typically, the oven and dishwasher are part of the sale, with the fridge and microwave being optional. However, in today's kitchens, because fridges are so big and microwaves are built-in, both are usually part of the package. The listing for the home will state what is included, but they are not always 100% accurate as the listing agent could have made an error in noting certain details regarding the home. Two items that may be included are the washer and dryer. Usually people take these with them when they move; however, if you want them, ask for them to be included in the price. You will never get what you don't ask for, so it does not hurt to make a request. You are also welcome to ask for furniture or anything else you see that you would like.

Your real estate agent will go over all of this and more in detail. Agents specialize in writing the offer and for that reason will be of great help to you. The agent will also help you to come up with a price to offer. It's common practice to offer less than the asking price. However, if there is demand for the property you are interested in, that property could receive multiple offers at the same time, in which case, the higher offer will prevail. In such cases, the final price is often higher than the listed price of the home. Exercise caution in these situations so you don't find yourself committing to a home priced higher than one you would be comfortable with. Again, your agent will help you make your offer. He/she will also be able to share comparative sales with you so you have an idea of what similar homes have sold for in recent months.

Your offer will be limited to and/or influenced by:

- Your budget / pre-approval amount

- Your desire for the home
- Sale prices of comparable homes
- Market demand for the home of interest
- The seller's motivation to sell
- The length of time the seller has been trying to sell the home (time on market)
- Improvements required to bring the home up-to-date
- Property taxes and association dues

There is nothing wrong with making your first offer a "low ball" offer. This will give you an idea as to how motivated the seller is. They may have their home listed at a price higher than the market with the hopes of getting a more median price, so you should start low to see. If they don't like your offer, you will find out from your real estate agent because the seller will either come back with a "no" or a counter offer. Sometimes you might go back and forth a number of times before both sides settle on a price.

In some neighborhoods, you may not be able to negotiate for a lower price since a number of buyers may want that property. For this reason, the seller will end up getting a higher price than the one at which they had listed the home. I have seen this to be the case in certain neighborhoods in the city of Chicago.

You make your money when you buy your real estate, not when you sell it. Don't get too excited over a property that is in the midst of a bidding war as you may find yourself overpaying and regretting it later. Just remember to keep the concepts of the financial benefits of real estate in the back of your mind.

Furthermore, in making the offer, the more you know about the seller's reasons for selling, the more ammunition you have for negotiating. If you can hit their hot buttons, you may find yourself negotiating for a better price or getting some extras, such as appliances and/or furniture included in the price.

To give you an idea of how sellers can act and react, let me recount a scenario for you. One of my clients wanted to purchase a home from a seller who had lived in the home for many years and who wanted it to go to a "worthy" buyer. Typically, a closing is completed within 60 days or less, but because the seller really liked my client, they were willing to wait just about four months to close so that my client could finish the lease on her apartment. My point in telling you this story is that you never know a seller's thoughts or intentions, but if you keep an open mind and act fairly, the seller may be kind in return.

Contingencies

Your offer to purchase will more than likely contain some contingencies. Contingencies are conditions that must be satisfied by the seller, or you will not be required to complete the purchase of the home. Make mental or written notes of visible problems when you're looking at the home for the first time. Some things to watch for are misaligned siding, cracked drywall, cracked floor tiles, a botched-up lawn, wet spots on the foundation walls in the basement, wet/discolored spots on wood-finished basement walls, missing shingles on the roof, etc.; these are all negotiation points when making an offer to support a lower price.

(Keep in mind that you will have a home inspection after the seller agrees to the contract and your home inspector will point out major faults you have not identified on your own that should be corrected. Once the home inspection is completed, you will indicate to your attorney any major faults you want the seller to correct. These faults will become additional contingencies on your real estate contract. Your attorney will then negotiate with the seller's attorney on the issues you have pointed out.)

Just remember: if the seller does not want to fix anything and does not want to budge on the price, you might want to consider moving on to a different home since you could go broke trying to fix things to bring the home up-to-date.

An example of a contingency would be that your offer is subject to the seller repairing the potholes in the driveway or giving credit to make the repairs yourself. In this case, if the seller did not want to complete the repairs or provide credit, you would have the right to withdraw your offer to purchase.

Your offer will be contingent on a variety of issues, which I have summed up here:

- Securing satisfactory financing
- Attorney review of the offer to purchase
- Satisfactory home inspection
- Satisfactory well and septic tests
- Satisfactory radon tests
- Getting a certificate of occupancy from the village for the property (new construction)
- Obtaining an appraisal with the value supporting the purchase price
- Repairs that you have asked the seller to make
- A closing date that meets your timetable, e.g., rental lease expiring, etc.

Other contingencies may be applicable as they relate to your specific situation. Your attorney and real estate agent will help you with this. Remember, if the seller fails to meet the contingencies set forth in the contract, you have the option to withdraw your offer to purchase and walk away from the transaction without penalty.

Earnest Money

When you are sitting down with your real estate agent to write up the contract, you will also be required to write out a check for what is known as earnest money. This is your deposit to show the seller your good faith.

If your purchase closes, your earnest money will be identified and deducted on the closing statement for the transaction. If your purchase does not go through because the seller rejected your offer or failed to perform their part of the contract, you would be entitled to a full refund of your earnest money. If you fail to perform your part of the contract, and then decide to back out of the purchase, you may not be entitled to this refund.

Your real estate agent will advise you on the customary amount of earnest money you will need. Keep in mind that if you gave $5,000 as earnest money, that $5,000 would be applied as a credit at closing on the closing statement toward your down payment and/or closing costs.

Counter offers

Once you make an offer to the seller, they can accept it as is, reject it, or make a counter offer. If you make a very low offer, the seller has the right to not even respond, which I have seen happen. However, their real estate agent will try to talk them into responding in some way as a sign of good faith in negotiating, even though you may have put out a really low and insulting offer.

In a counter offer, the seller has the right to change any of the terms of your offer. For example, they can come back with a higher price, they can delete some or all of your contingencies, or they can do anything they want as part of the negotiation so the terms meet their demands.

The odds are that you will receive a counter offer from the seller, so you have the same options to accept it, reject it, or make another counter offer. This is the stressful part of negotiating the purchase of a home. You could go back and forth numerous times before you reach an agreement on the price and terms.

This negotiation process could happen in one day or could span a few days or more. Most of this negotiation after the initial written offer will be between your agent and the seller's agent by phone. Once they have some final results, they will modify your existing offer to purchase and have you initial the changes. At that point, your agent will fax over a copy to the seller's agent for the seller to initial and sign off on.

Even after you have reached an agreement, you will still have to take a few more steps since you will have only five business days to take care of some issues. (As you recall, the 5-day period could vary by state or county, so for the purposes of this book, I will be using 5 days.) This is why knowing who your attorney and home inspector are in advance will make this part of the buying process less hectic.

The steps that will take place once the contract is signed are:

- Fax or email a copy of the contract to your attorney for review (five business days).
- Fax or email a copy of the contract to your mortgage professional.
- Order a home inspection (five business days).
- Order other inspections as necessary — your agent will advise you on this (five business days):
  - radon tests
  - well and septic tests
  - other tests.
- The mortgage professional will order an appraisal for the property from the lender.

Once all of these steps have been completed, you could expect to wait 45 to 90 days before you close and pick up the keys to your new home.

Entering Escrow

In some states, once you have a contract, you enter into escrow. The escrow company holds the earnest money in trust and ensures the demands contained within the contract are carried out. The escrow company also provides the settlement services (closing) for the exchange of money between the buyer, seller, and lender. In most states the settlement services are provided by the title company and the earnest money is held in trust by the listing agent's real estate company. Your real estate agent will know which process your state uses.

Mortgage Contingency

The contract you sign will have a mortgage contingency date. This is the date by which the seller wants to know when you will be approved for the loan. The mortgage contingency date is often 3 to 4 weeks after the date of the contract. This is another reason that it is very important to be pre-approved prior to going out shopping for a home as the mortgage professional will have limited time to fulfill this contractual obligation on your behalf. If you do not meet this contingency date, the seller will have the right to keep your earnest money deposit and put the property back on the market for sale.

What if the Closing Date Has To Be Pushed Back?

Your real estate agent will set an estimated closing date when you complete the offer to purchase. You can revise the date later if the conditions are such that all interested parties are ready to close the transaction early. One reason for a postponed closing date is that the lender does not have the loan fully approved yet. This could be because of delays from your providing support information, backlogs at the lender, appraisal issues, or other snags. In most cases, loans close on time, but just be aware that certain circumstances could cause a delay.

If you have been renting and your lease is going to expire, pushing the closing date back could put you in a homeless situation for a brief period if your landlord is not able to accommodate an extension to your lease. When you are making your offer to the seller, make sure you talk with your real estate agent about picking a closing date at least 45 to 60 days out from the date of the contract to allow enough time for the lending process. I have seen rush situations from a short closing timeframe that caused a lot of stress for the client and real estate agents when things didn't flow perfectly and dates had to be pushed back.

The Appraisal

After all of your tests and inspections have been completed and the attorney review is satisfactory, it will be time for your mortgage professional to order the appraisal to verify the home's value. The appraisal will be ordered usually within that 5-day period, although it is not a requirement that the appraisal be completed within that 5-day window. Usually the appraisal takes up to two weeks to be completed.

The purpose of the appraisal is to determine the value of your home as compared to other similar homes in the immediate area. The appraisal is required by the lender to ensure your new home will support the amount of money you are borrowing. The appraiser will go to the home and take a variety of measurements and make evaluations of the lot, home size, room sizes, the quality of cabinets, flooring, finished rooms, and many other areas. The appraiser will then compare the home to other similar homes in the area to come up with a value. If the home you are buying has certain upgrades other homes do not have, you could expect the value of your home to be worth more. The same can be true for the reverse.

If for any reason the value of the appraisal comes in significantly lower than the agreed upon price you have in your contract, you have the right to go back to the seller and advise them that their home was overpriced. The seller can then decide to work with you to agree on the lower price, or you have the option to terminate the contract. Your real estate agent and attorney will be helpful in this area as well.

The appraiser will schedule a time with the seller's real estate agent to visually inspect the property. You are not allowed to attend the appraiser's inspection. Once the inspection is completed, the appraiser will submit to the lender his/her report, which is a universal form (1004 Universal Appraisal). The lender will advise the mortgage professional and you of the appraised value. The lender will then review your appraisal as part of the process for approving your loan.

Home Warranty

When you are purchasing an existing home, you might want to obtain a home warranty to cover major repairs during your first year of ownership. For example, when I bought my house, I obtained a home warranty. Within the first year, my water heater was leaking and had to be replaced. My cost was the $60 service fee for the technician. The warranty company paid for the rest. This saved me quite a bit of money and made the cost of the policy worthwhile.

As a homebuyer, your goal is to get the seller to pay for the home warranty. The cost is roughly $300 to $500 for one year, but could be more if you have a significantly higher-priced home. Some real estate agents will automatically offer a home warranty. In the case of my first home, my real estate agent surprised me with it as a gift at closing. I had no idea what a home warranty was when I was buying a home, but it was a nice surprise after I learned about its purpose. It came in handy when I had a problem in my first home that needed to be corrected.

When you sit down to make your offer, ask your real estate agent about a home warranty, and then ask for the seller to pay for the warranty as part of your offer.

Picking a Lender and Submitting Your Loan Application

Now that you have found a home, your mortgage professional can officially submit your loan application to an underwriter at a lender for approval. Your mortgage professional will pick a lender that he or she feels will be the best lender for your borrowing circumstances and the best lender to meet certain dates contained in your real estate contract. When you complete your real estate contract, there will be a mortgage contingency date, which is the date you need to receive a formal approval from the lender for your new loan. Your mortgage professional will want to select a lender who can meet that date so you ensure that you fulfill your contractual obligations.

Locking Your Interest Rate

After you find a home and have a contract, it's now time to have a discussion with your mortgage professional about locking an interest rate at the lender your loan has been submitted to. In your initial meeting with your mortgage professional, you would have talked about interest rates. Ideally, when you were pre-approved, your mortgage professional used a higher interest rate to qualify you for the loan so that in the event interest rates went up once you found a home, you were still able to qualify.

As I talked about earlier in this book, interest rates can and do change almost daily. The downside you face as a homebuyer is that you are not able to lock your interest rate in until you have found a home and have a contract for purchase. Locking an interest rate means that the lender will guarantee you that interest rate when you close. If your rate is not locked, your interest rate will float and you are subject to higher or lower interest rates as the market changes. Once you lock the rate, you have that rate regardless if rates go up or down.

When interest rates are quoted, they are quoted based on a 30-day lock period. The decision to lock is yours. This is just one more reason that you want to be working with an experienced mortgage professional who can shed some light on what is going on in the marketplace so that you are properly informed and can make the right decision about locking. If interest rates are low and you may not be closing on your home for 45 days, you will have to pay extra for a 45- or 60-day lock if you decide to lock at that time. Different lenders have different lock periods, so you will have to lock within their parameters. Some will have only 30-, 60-, and 90-day locks. Others will have 15-,30-, 45-, 60-, and 90-day locks. Costs to lock will vary slightly by lender as well. Your mortgage professional will let you know the costs to lock your loan beyond 30 days. Bear in mind that this will be additional money you will have to bring to the closing table. Your mortgage strategy combined with current market conditions for interest rates will dictate when you decide to lock.

CHAPTER 9
The Closing

The day you close on the purchase of your new home will be a big day. A month or two would have passed since you signed your contract for purchase, and all your possessions will have been packed. At this point, you will be ready to move! You will be a bundle of nerves as all of the stress, thought, and preparation of homebuying will be coming to an end. The closing is the last step in this long homebuying process. The purpose of the closing is to settle the transaction.

The closing will take place at a title company's office with a closing agent or at an escrow company with an escrow agent. Sometimes the closing can take place remotely in the office of an attorney, real estate agent, or the mortgage company where a representative from the title or escrow company be present. You can expect the closing to last anywhere from thirty minutes to two hours. Some closings go smoothly; others may be a bit more difficult as there may be errors that have to be corrected (e.g., sometimes the wire transfer (money) from the lender is late, among other delays). So you will need to be patient.

If you have children, sometimes it's best to have somebody watch them while you attend the closing because they might get a little restless during a long one. At most closings I have attended, the title company (which is where loans usually close in Illinois) did not have toys or games to occupy the children while the closing was taking place.

In general, those in attendance will be you, your attorney, the seller's attorney, and the respective real estate agents. The seller alone does not have to attend the closing because they can pre-sign their papers and, on their behalf, their attorney can take care of any issues that may arise. In my experience, the seller has come to 50% of the closings I have attended. The mortgage professional does not have to attend the closing, but many do.

During the closing, you will be signing a lot of papers, all of which your attorney or closing agent will go over in detail with you. Most of the documents you sign will be related to the loan you have taken out.

Title Companies and Title Insurance

The role of a title company is to provide title insurance for the property that is being purchased or refinanced. Title insurance is a one-time insurance policy for which you have to pay when you purchase or refinance a home. The purpose of this insurance is to protect you and your lender from past claims against the land your home is on. The records for your land are typically kept in the county in which your home is located. Whenever land changes hands or lenders, mistakes can happen in the recording of the information. Also, fraud can occur when it is discovered that someone, for example, had forged a signature on a deed claiming ownership of the land. The purpose of the title company is to ensure the title they are providing you and the lender is clean and that any errors or future claims of ownership the title company failed to clear will be the financial responsibility of the title insurance company should something surface in the future. This insuring is done via the title insurance policy for which you are paying.

The secondary service the title company provides, if you are not in an escrow state, is settlement services for purchase or refinance transactions. They will compile the financial numbers related to a purchase or refinance transaction and then disperse the funds to close the transaction.

The Day of Closing – Final Walkthrough

On the day you close (or sometimes the night before) you and your real estate agent will do a final walkthrough of the home you are buying. Some time will have passed since you last saw the home, so you will just want to check it is still in the same condition it was when you agreed to purchase it. Moreover, if anything had to be repaired as a result of the home inspection, this will be your chance to make certain these items have indeed been repaired. (In any case, the seller will need to provide proof with paid receipts at closing, showing the items had been repaired.)

By now the seller will have moved out, and you will notice some things you had not noticed before because the house is now empty. You may see fading of paint on walls where pictures were hanging, nail holes, and marks and scuffs previously covered up by furniture. These minor flaws are ok; they are normal wear-and-tear of the home. Feel free to check appliances, the furnace, the air conditioner, and the toilets to ensure they are all in working order. In addition, check that the items the seller agreed to leave behind (such as furniture, appliances, etc.) as part of the contract are still there. If they have been removed, you must let your attorney know so you can either get them back or have the value deducted from the sales/purchase price.

You will also want to make sure the seller has moved all of their personal possessions out of the home. When I bought my last home, the seller still had belongings there on the morning of the closing. I advised my attorney of this, who then made it clear to the seller that the items had to be removed by the end of business that day or they would incur rental costs for the items still in the house, a house that was now mine. The seller came by later in the day to remove the items and to give us the keys, which they neglected to give to their attorney at closing. (My wife and I were able to get into our house since the sliding door lock was bad—a unique way to enter one's new home for the first time!)

What to Bring to the Closing

There are only a few things you need to bring to the closing. By this point, everything else will have already been taken care of. You should make sure to have:

1. A hazard insurance paid receipt
2. A certified or cashier's check for down payment and closing costs
3. Your driver's license / state ID and Social Security card

Hazard insurance paid receipt

As part of the closing, the title insurance agent will verify that you have paid your insurance to satisfy that requirement on the lender's behalf. (If you are buying a condominium-type property for which you do not have to have your own homeowner's policy, you will not need to worry about this as the lender will have obtained a copy of the policy for the complex prior to closing). The loan processer who works with the mortgage professional you are using will often request that you fax him/her a copy of your paid receipt prior to closing; however, it's always important to bring your original copy from your agent with you in the event some paperwork gets mixed up. Just as a reminder: you will have to pay a full year's worth of homeowner's insurance (hazard insurance) before you close.

Certified or cashier's check

On the day before closing, the mortgage professional will contact you to give you a final amount of how much money you will need to bring to closing. As I have mentioned earlier, you may be receiving certain credits from the seller or your prepaid items (taxes, insurance & prepaid interest) will change if your closing date has changed. So, the actual amount you thought you needed might change. Once you have the final amount, head over to your bank to obtain a certified check or cashier's check. Make sure you tell the bank to make the check payable to you. The reason for this is that if there is a problem with the closing, you can always easily redeposit that check back into your account. At the closing table, you will endorse the check when the title insurance agent asks you to do so.

Keep in mind that the final tally of numbers is not completed by the closing agent until a day or two before closing. So just be prepared to go at the last minute to your bank to get your check prior to closing. If, for whatever reason, you are not able to obtain your check after receiving the final amount, you can always obtain it in advance for a ballpark figure to bring with you to the closing. The mortgage professional can give you this ballpark figure based on their estimates. If the amount of the check you obtained is for too much, the closing agent will provide you with a refund at the closing. Most mortgage professionals will estimate high so you don't have to worry about being short money when you arrive to the closing.

Your driver's license / state ID and Social Security card

To provide proof of your identity at closing, you should bring along your driver's license or state ID along with your Social Security card.

Get Ready to Start Signing

As I mentioned earlier, be prepared to do a lot of signing of paperwork. You may feel as if you are signing your life away, but in reality it's not that bad. In this section, I have listed the most important documents that you will be signing. In addition, you will be signing others that are related to the title insurance and updated copies of your original loan application, among others. The most important documents you will be signing are:

- The mortgage note
- The Mortgage / Deed of Trust
- The Deed
- HUD -1 Settlement Statement

The Mortgage Note

The mortgage note is your promise to repay the loan for your new home. It is also known as a promissory note. The note outlines the terms of your new loan, including the amount financed, interest rate, payment, and the date the loan is due.

The Mortgage / Deed of Trust

The mortgage is the pledging of your home as security for the loan. In the event you default on your mortgage note, the mortgage gives the rights to the lender to take your home away from you using the process of fore-closure.

The mortgage states that you will have the right to live in and use the home, but must pay the lender back. If you do not pay the lender back, the lender has the right to take the home away from you using the process of foreclosure. Once you have paid off your loan, you will receive the mortgage back from the lender as you now own the home free and clear. Sometimes you might hear people say that they can't wait to burn the mortgage. What they mean is that they can't wait to get their home paid off and burn the paper that pledged their home to the lender; it's a celebration of sorts.

After all, it is a big accomplishment to get your home paid off.

Depending on the state in which you live, a mortgage is also sometimes known as a Deed of Trust or Trust Deed. The basic concepts of a mortgage and deed of trust is the same except that a deed of trust involves a third party called a trustee (usually a title insurance company) who acts on behalf of the lender. When you sign a deed of trust, you are in effect giving the trustee the title (ownership) of the property, but holding onto the right to use and live in it.

States where you will find Deeds of Trust are:

> Alaska
> Arizona
> California
> Mississippi
> Missouri
> Nevada
> North Carolina
> Virginia
> Washington, D.C.

The remaining states not listed use just a mortgage or retain the option to use a Deed of Trust. It is not important for you to remember this information; you just need to be aware of it so when you hear the words from your attorney at closing and you are about to sign the document, you will have a rough understanding of what you are signing.

The Deed
The deed transfers legal ownership of the property from the seller to you, the buyer.

The HUD-1 Settlement Statement
The HUD-1 Settlement Statement, shown in *Figure 9-1* and *Figure 9-2*, is another standard form from the government, namely HUD. The state-

HUD-1 Settlement Statement (Page 1)

A. SETTLEMENT STATEMENT   U.S. DEPARTMENT OF HOUSING AND URBAN DEVELOPMENT

OMB NO. 2502-0265

B. TYPE OF LOAN

1. ☐ FHA	2. ☐ FmHA	3. ☐ CONV.UNINS.	6. File Number:	7. Loan Number:	8. Mortgage Insurance Case Number:
4. ☐ VA	5. ☐ CONV.INS.				

C. NOTE: This form is furnished to give you a statement of actual settlement costs. Amounts paid to and by the settlement agent are shown. Items marked "(p.o.c.)" were paid outside the closing; they are shown here for informational purposes and are not included in the totals.

D. NAME AND ADDRESS OF BORROWER:	E. NAME AND ADDRESS OF SELLER/TAX I.D. NO.:	F. NAME AND ADDRESS OF LENDER:

G. PROPERTY LOCATION:	H. SETTLEMENT AGENT:
	Disbursement Date:
	PLACE OF SETTLEMENT: I. SETTLEMENT DATE:

J. SUMMARY OF BORROWER'S TRANSACTION		K. SUMMARY OF SELLER'S TRANSACTION	
100. GROSS AMOUNT DUE FROM BORROWER:		**400. GROSS AMOUNT DUE TO SELLER:**	
101. Contract Sales Price		401. Contract Sales Price	
102. Personal Property		402. Personal Property	
103. Settlement charges to borrower (line 1400)		403.	
104.		404.	
105.		405.	
Adjustments for items paid by seller in advance		Adjustments for items paid by seller in advance	
106. City/town taxes to		406. City/town taxes to	
107. County taxes to		407. County taxes to	
108. Assessments to		408. Assessments to	
109.		409.	
110.		410.	
111.		411.	
112.		412.	
120. GROSS AMOUNT DUE FROM BORROWER		**420. GROSS AMOUNT DUE TO SELLER**	
200. AMOUNTS PAID BY OR IN BEHALF OF BORROWER:		500. REDUCTIONS IN AMOUNT DUE TO SELLER:	
201. Deposit or earnest money		501. Excess deposit (see instructions)	
202. Principal amount of new loan(s)		502. Settlement charges to seller (line 1400)	
203. Existing loan(s) taken subject to		503. Existing loan(s) taken subject to	
204.		504. Payoff of first mortgage loan	
205.		505. Payoff of second mortgage loan	
206.		506.	
207.		507.	
208.		508.	

Figure 9-1

ment lists all the financial costs and credits for the buyer, seller, lender(s), real estate agent(s), attorney(s), and other parties involved in this transaction. The statement will show the total amount required for you to bring to the closing table as well as how much money the seller is getting or owes after any loans and/or services have been paid for.

HUD-1 Settlement Statement (Page 2)

L. SETTLEMENT CHARGES			PAID FROM BORROWER'S FUNDS AT SETTLEMENT	PAID FROM SELLER'S FUNDS AT SETTLEMENT
700. TOTAL SALES/BROKER'S COMMISSION				
based on price $	@	%=		
Division of Commission (line 700) as follows:				
701. $	to			
702. $	to			
703. Commission paid at Settlement				
704.				
800. ITEMS PAYABLE IN CONNECTION WITH LOAN				
801. Loan Origination Fee	%			
802. Loan Discount	%			
803. Appraisal Fee to				
804. Credit Report to				
805. Lenders Inspection Fee				
806. Mortgage Insurance Application Fee to				
807. Assumption Fee				
808.				
809.				
810.				
811.				
900. ITEMS REQUIRED BY LENDER TO BE PAID IN ADVANCE				
901. Interest from	to	@$ /day		
902. Mortgage Insurance Premium for	months to			
903. Hazard Insurance Premium for	years to			
904. Flood Insurance Premium for	years to			
905.				
1000. RESERVES DEPOSITED WITH LENDER				
1001. Hazard Insurance	months @$	per month		
1002. Mortgage Insurance	months @$	per month		
1003. City property taxes	months @$	per month		
1004. County property taxes	months @$	per month		
1005. Annual assessments	months @$	per month		
1006. Flood insurance	months @$	per month		
1007. Aggregate Adjustment	months @$	per month		
1008.				
1100. TITLE CHARGES				
1101. Settlement or closing fee	to			
1102. Abstract or title search	to			
1103. Title examination	to			
1104. Title insurance binder	to			
1105. Document preparation	to			
1106. Notary fees	to			
1107. Attorney's fees	to			
(includes above items numbers:		)		
1108. Title Insurance	to			
(includes above items numbers:		)		
1109. Lender's coverage	$			
1110. Owner's coverage	$			
1111.				
1112				

Figure 9-2

The HUD-1 Settlement Statement will be the last document you have to sign at the closing. After you sign it, the title agent will collect your check and begin to disburse funds to the respective parties. At this point, the seller's attorney will hand over the keys to your new home.

You Are Officially a Homeowner

Congratulations! You are now living the American dream of home-ownership. Soon you will be on your way to creating wealth with your new home.

PART III

LIFE AS A HOMEOWNER

CHAPTER 10
After the Closing

After you become a homeowner, you need to take steps to make the best of this experience. Protecting your net worth includes maintaining the value of your home through proper upkeep and having the right insurance protection. By not keeping your home in working order, you will find that the cost of repairs will be even more expensive than if you made repairs immediately. Furthermore, without protecting your investment with insurance, you are at risk of losing everything should a catastrophe occur. Without the proper coverage, you could find yourself in financial ruin.

Maintaining Your Home

No matter what type of home you own, things are bound to break and malfunction. It's very important to fix broken items immediately because once things break, they have a tendency to worsen if left in disrepair. For example, when a rock hits your windshield, the point of impact on the glass usually starts out with a small crack. Then, that crack grows until you have no choice but to get the window replaced. Had you gone to the glass repair company right away, you might have been able to stop the crack from growing—repairing the window would have been much cheaper than buying an entirely new one. The same principle applies to areas in your home. Cracked tile will deteriorate; a small leak will turn into a big leak. As problems worsen, the cost of repairs will be greater. Your best bet is to nip those problems in the bud as soon as you can. Even if you merely suspect there is a problem, get it checked out. If you are buying a newer home, you will not have as many repair issues, but I have seen newer homes with problems because the previous homeowner did not properly maintain the home.

One way to save a lot of money is to learn how to perform basic repairs yourself. Tune in to home improvement TV shows to see how homeowners are fixing things on their own. Another valuable resource that I myself have found useful is a giant orange book from Home Depot titled, Home Improvement 1-2-3. This book is also available in bookstores. The best parts are the detailed lists of tools you need and the pictures showing you how to perform specific repairs.

In my own home, I have done 85% of the remodeling work just from learning what I watched on TV, reading the Home Depot book, and getting tips from my father-in-law. Not only do I enjoy the projects, but I have saved myself thousands of dollars in labor costs! In your case, you have to decide if the repairs are worth your time and energy. If the problem is bigger than you are willing or able to tackle, it might make more sense to pay someone to fix it instead of acquiring the tools and setting the time aside to fix it yourself. One thing you will learn is that if you think it will take you 20 minutes to fix something, it may actually take you double that time. If you prefer to hire out, I advise you to ask around to find an inexpensive, but reliable handyman or handywoman who serves as a jack-of-all-trades. You can ask your real estate agent, mortgage professional, or attorney for a reference of a handyman or handywoman.

The main point here is that you must maintain all areas of your home to minimize your cost of owning.

Improving Your Home

Naturally, most homeowners want to improve their home according to their own taste and style. Such improvements could include new flooring, cabinets, tile, countertops and so on. Improving your home can be good or bad depending on the quality of the work that has been performed or the types of improvements that have been made.

Remember that part of the goal of homeownership is to improve your net worth through appreciation. One thing to avoid is over-improving your home. That might sound illogical, but as you begin to contemplate making improvements, consider the neighborhood in which you live and what a homebuyer who would be buying a home in your neighborhood may be looking for. It's very easy to overinflate the value of your home with significant improvements. So, if you plan on purchasing a home to then renovate or improve upon it, in my opinion, it would be wise to purchase a home that is outdated and below market value. In this way, when you finish with the improvements, your home will be at market value or slightly above it.

For example, in my 20-year-old home, some of the windows leak air (making it a little drafty in the winter months). I have begun to look for replacement windows. An acquaintance recommended that I install a well-known, high-end brand of windows. With top quality, name-brand windows, however, comes a higher price tag. In the neighborhood in which I live, lavish improvements would not be financially beneficial for the price range of my home. Someone buying a significantly more expensive home than mine would be concerned with the type and brand of windows in the home. The more expensive a home is, the higher the expectations are in terms of quality of materials and appliances. I can still find a good quality window for my home, but at a much more affordable price that would be compatible with the neighborhood. I have nothing against a higher-end brand of windows, but in my case, it would take quite a few years of appreciation to realize the benefit of installing them.

Let's say you buy a home for $300,000 and put $30,000 into it; you want to at least get more than $330,000 when you sell the house. But bear in mind, you still have to account for the cost of the real estate agent to sell your home. So though you put $30,000 into it, you have to add another $21,000 in this case to break even to cover the realtor's commission. Otherwise, you have really gained nothing in the area of appreciation, and you are not seeing a return on the investment you made. You enjoyed the home more as a result of the improvements, but you did nothing for your net worth.

In the case of your first home, you typically want to transfer the equity that has been created through appreciation into a second home you may purchase 5 to 7 years down the road. By doing so, the larger home will be more affordable. If you truly earned $30,000 in appreciation, that is $30,000 more you can put toward the newer home. *Figure 10-1* analyzes this concept.

Let me give you another example. At the time that I was writing this book, I had just recently finished my basement. I could have gone into extreme improvement mode making the basement lavish with a wet bar, digging up the basement floor to put in plumbing for a toilet and shower, and

Break-Even Sales Analysis		
Purchase price of home		$300,000
Improvements made to home	+	$30,000
Sale price to break even	=	$330,000
Real estate commission at 6%	+	$21,000
Actual price for which you must sell home to break even	=	**$351,000**

Figure 10-1

using extravagant woods and moldings. I know my wife and I would have enjoyed some of these features as it would have made for a great space to entertain. But once again, these improvements would not have been financially beneficial considering the price range of our home. So, I kept the design fairly basic, and now we still have a comfortable basement that fits the rest of the house in terms of style. As a result, for an affordable price I was able to complete the basement, which will still bring me value when I'm ready to sell.

When you are considering improvements to your home, you always want to keep two things in mind:

1. Will the improvement enhance my quality of life?
2. Will the improvement bring me a return when I sell?

When considering improvements, again be cautious in your choice of materials since it is very easy to overspend. For example, do you need the high-end ceramic tile or would a more affordable, similar version work?

Don't buy something just to be able to keep up with your neighbors and brag that you have it—this is merely self-indulgence. In reality, nobody really cares what you have. On the other hand, if you are living in a million dollar plus home, then some of those expensive brand names will be expected because a buyer with more expensive tastes will be looking for a house with designer embellishments.

Let's look at one final example about over-improving. I enjoy a TV show called the "Million Dollar Listing" on the Bravo channel. Set in the Los Angeles area, the show is a real-life depiction of the careers of three young real estate agents. In one of the episodes, one of the agents takes a listing from a seller who improved his condo, turning it into an extraordinarily beautiful place. As a result, the seller thought the home was worth more than what the agent thought it was worth. Against the agent's better judgment, the agent agreed with the seller and listed the condo at the higher price. During the Realtor® open house (which is an open house for real estate agents to view new homes on the market), all of the agents commented that the home was overpriced and would be difficult to sell. However, the seller did not want to lower his price, and the home ended up not getting sold.

According to most real estate agents and appraisers I speak with, to create value in your home, improving a few key areas will bring you the best return for your dollars spent:

- Kitchen
- Master bath
- Landscaping – curb appeal
- Flooring

Kitchen

Again, stay in line with the expectations for your neighborhood or condo building. On upgrading a kitchen, you could spend $5,000 to $100,000. But is your home worth a $100,000 kitchen? It might be, if it's in an area where houses have kitchens that expensive. In my case, I was able to upgrade my kitchen for $7,000 (including new appliances) and did most of the work myself, saving close to $3,000 in labor costs. Mine looks like a nice kitchen that you would find in a brand new home, but was completed in a way that is compatible with the other homes in the neighborhood. In any case, my wife and I are pleased with how it looks, and we love cooking, eating, and entertaining in our new space.

Master Bath

Owners love their master bathroom, so this is a part of the home that is worth improving. You can also affordably improve this area. Home improvement stores sell good quality and reasonably priced fixtures, vanities, toilets, and towel rods to improve a bathroom's appearance. At the same time, you could spend thousands improving a master bath by using a firm to do major design work. I have seen bathroom improvements in excess of $30,000 for one bathroom. However, I have also seen improvements for less than $2,000. If you are budget-conscious, it's amazing how you can change the look and feel of a bathroom for a reasonable price. Again, the value placed on the improvement is all relative to the expectations of a homebuyer who is looking in your area.

Landscaping – Curb Appeal

Having curb appeal will definitely improve your home's value and make it easier to sell. Unfortunately, shrubs and bushes tend to get a bit overgrown after 20 years and may need to be replaced. Simply replacing bushes and maintaining your yard will go a long way in improving the value of your home. The biggest mistake people make with their landscaping is not controlling the growth of shrubs and bushes. When these become overgrown, a yard looks dated and shabby. The more expensive your home is, the higher the expectation will be regarding the type and complexity of landscaping. Always keep your yard in good shape to keep up with the neighborhood. You will feel proud when you see your home from the street, and your neighbors will appreciate it too since you are helping maintain the quality of the neighborhood.

If you are considering doing some landscape improvements, you'll be surprised to learn that it's a much easier task to accomplish than you might think. When I bought my house, the back and south sides of the house did not have any shrubs. The grass from the yard extended right up to the foundation of the house. Needless to say, the house was not very appealing from those angles. After doing some research, reading some books, and talking to a couple of different local nurseries, my wife and I were able to decide on some shrubs to plant; these were going to grow to a size that would be appropriate for the space. We initially were going to hire out to get the work done until I realized it was simple; all I needed to do was dig a hole and add some peat moss to prepare the ground for planting. We brought most of the shrubs home ourselves, but had some of the bigger ones delivered. We set aside a couple of Saturdays to get to work and we did the planting ourselves. Out of 17 shrubs planted, we only had one that didn't make it. Had we not shredded our receipt, we would have been able to replace the dying shrub for free since the shrubs came with a one-year warranty from the nursery. Needless to say, while it was a lot of hard work, we felt immense satisfaction at seeing the result. Besides, it was fun working on this project together.

One word of caution before you dig. Before you start digging in your yard, check with your local municipality about a service offered that will come out and mark where your various underground utilities are so that you do not accidently cut or damage them when you begin digging. Most of these services are offered for free, so you will want to check with the city you live in. This service will mark your yard for gas, electric, water, sewer, cable, and telephone. Even if you are just going to plant some small bushes, give them a call. The last thing you want to do is damage one of those lines, which could end up costing you a lot to repair. [In the Chicago area, the service is usually advertised as "Call JULIE Before You Dig." (JULIE stands for "Joint Utility Locating Information for Excavators.")]

Flooring

Would you rather buy a home that has all vinyl flooring or would you rather have a home with hardwood floors or ceramic tile? Earlier I mentioned I bought my home at a slight discount compared to other recent sales in my neighborhood. One of the reasons for this discount is that the carpet was 20 years old and the kitchen and bathrooms had vinyl flooring. As I mentioned before, I redid the kitchen. When I was choosing flooring, I could have kept the vinyl, put down a laminate fake wood (which is like vinyl to me), or put down ¾" hardwood floors. I chose the ¾" hardwood because of its longevity since it can be refinished a few times during its life far beyond my ownership. The hardwood was roughly twice as much as the laminate wood floor would have been, but the wood improved the value of my home more so than the laminate would have.

Since flooring does add value to your home, be wise in the choices you make. If you are budget-conscious and select cheap solutions that a prospective buyer may not like, it could take you longer to sell the home and bring you less return on your investment. In my case, I selected middle-of-the-road solutions for my hardwood floors and carpet.

Watch the Spending

I have touched on this before but again want to point out that after you acquire your home, you need to be careful of your spending. It's very easy to rack up credit card debt by going out and buying new furniture and doing home improvements. The one thought people have is, I will charge it all now and then pay it off later. But with some credit cards charging 10% plus interest rates, people find that paying off credit card debt takes longer than they thought. And as other issues in life come up that require money— money that is supposed to go toward paying off the credit card bills—there is less to go around to cover all of your costs. Save and plan for your projects so you can pay for most of them in cash.

If you have ever struggled to hold yourself back from making certain purchases, I suggest you watch The Suze Orman Show on CNBC. She has a segment on the show called Can I Afford It? In it, people call in with an item they want to purchase such as a new fur coat, boats, swing sets, trips they want to take, etc. Ms. Orman gathers their financial background, analyzes the numbers, and then lets them know, in her professional opinion, if she thinks they can afford to make the purchase or not. Watching this segment is not only entertaining because of some of the things people want to buy, but also enlightening because it will really make you double-check your own situation. As a result of watching Suze Orman's show, my wife and I end up asking ourselves the "Can I afford it?" question when contemplating a potential purchase.

Don't Open up New Credit Cards

Another poor choice is to go out and open up a handful of "No Interest / No Payment" credit cards to fund improvements or buy furniture. While this type of credit card is good if you pay it off by the time the bill comes due, you need to be conscious of what opening up credit cards may do to your credit score, which you learned about in Chapter 6. If you open up too many, your credit score may drop. You should have only three to four credit cards at one time, so don't become overzealous in obtaining new ones. However, there may be situations in which you need to open up one of these cards, so let me share with you a strategy to do so wisely.

If you are married, let one spouse open up one card while the other spouse opens up another. Avoid opening them up jointly as you will have then added two cards to each of your credit reports rather than just one. Choose one card offer that might be most appropriate for what you are doing. For example, if you know you are going to be spending a lot of money at Home Depot, it may be worthwhile to open up a Home Depot card if they are offering incentives.

I share this with you because I have seen people come back to me with a lot of credit card debt after buying a home and they can't figure out why their credit scores have dropped. They are in a position in which they need to refinance to take out some money to pay down credit cards to improve their cash flow. The problem is that because their credit scores have dropped, their interest rate on the new mortgage loan is much higher than the original interest rate they had when they bought the home.

When my wife and I bought our current home, we needed to install all new carpeting and new floors in the kitchen. This was going to cost us nearly $6,000. We did not want to take money from savings to pay for this outright, but at the same time, we knew we needed to get this done before moving our furniture in. So, my wife and I decided to open up a card with the flooring retailer with whom we were working; they offered twelve months of no interest and no payments. We then took the cost of what we charged on the new card and divided it by twelve and made the twelve monthly payments on the balance. We knew going in that we could afford the monthly payment on the balance, pay off the balance within twelve months, and avoid paying the exorbitant interest charges. In our case, this was a perfect situation for us to open up one of these cards as we were able to make a large purchase and preserve our savings account at the same time.

Keep in mind that many of these no interest/no payments cards have a high interest rate attached. If you do not pay the balance off when the twelve months or advertised timeline has ended, the interest will be charged for the previous twelve months on the entire balance. Thus, you could see one-third or more added to your balance. Be careful, read the fine print, and know what you are getting into. I have met with people who did not pay the balance in time and found that their balance increased significantly because the interest kicked in. *Figure 10-2* outlines an example of a twelve-month, no interest/no payment credit card offer.

Zero Interest / No Payment Credit Card Scenario	
Original balance with your purchase	$3,000
Interest rate	22.90%
Term of offer	12 months
Interest added if balance not paid in full in 12 months	**$687**

Regardless of how much you have paid, if you do not pay the entire balance by the end of the twelve months, the full $687 of interest is added for which you are responsible. Make sure you fully understand the terms of the offer.

Figure 10-2

Protecting Your Investment – Insurance

A big mistake I see many people make is not having the correct insurance coverage. In the event that something catastrophic happens to your home, you could be out thousands of dollars and, as a result, find yourself in financial hardship because of those unexpected costs. Insurance coverage for your home is an absolute necessity and is well worth the cost.

Like many people, I did not thoroughly read the insurance policy I took out on my home. As I was in the process of finishing my basement in 2008, I called my agent to double-check exactly what my insurance policy covered. I started to think about all of the money, time, and hard work that I was putting into the basement and how it could all be severely damaged or completely destroyed if some disaster took place from flooding. I soon discovered when speaking to my insurance agent that if my basement flooded as a result of the sewer backing up, my sump pump giving out, or a wall cracking, the insurance would not cover it. The unfortunate part of this is that my insurance agent did not raise these issues when I was taking out the policy nor did I think to ask the questions. Had I not discovered this omission and had something catastrophic occurred, I would not have been covered by my insurance policy. As a result, I learned of the types of coverage available and selected one appropriate to protect my basement.

The type of insurance you obtain can make a huge difference in your out-of-pocket costs and what the insurance company would have to cover if something were to happen. Having solid coverage will also give you peace of mind. There are some people who do not want to invest a lot of thought or money when it comes to purchasing an insurance policy. However, by not doing so, the consequence could be large expenses. For example, an acquaintance of mine went with a cheaper insurance company, one for which she did not have a local agent with whom she worked; rather, if she had a problem, she had to call a toll-free phone number to the insurance company's call center. Unfortunately, she had an incident for which she needed to file a claim to have some repairs made, but found the whole process stressful and overwhelming as she had to deal with the representatives in the call center. Furthermore, she experienced delays in being reimbursed for the repairs that had to be completed. She spent a lot of unnecessary time trying to get the issues resolved. To avoid such headaches, my advice is to work with a local individual insurance agent and not necessarily go with a company because they have the cheapest rates. Be sure you have a local agent whom you can call when you have a problem or when you have questions that need to be answered promptly. Such service will give you peace of mind. When an accident or other incident does occur, that agent will go to bat for you to ensure your problems are taken care of.

In this next section, I want to make you aware of some of the insurance coverages available. However, when in doubt, always ask your agent if you have reservations about certain coverages. Depending on where you live in the country, different coverages are available for certain natural disasters. Earlier in the book I mentioned various types of insurance; I will elaborate in more detail in the pages ahead.

Homeowner's Insurance

As I said earlier in this book, when you buy a home, the lender is going to require that you obtain a homeowner's insurance policy. Typically you will have to pay for this insurance policy upfront to cover an entire year. Knowing this in advance will give you the opportunity to shop around and find the best insurance company and the best local agent and to identify a policy that will best suit your insurance needs. Remember, too, that if you are purchasing a condominium or townhome as opposed to a single-family home, your homeowner's insurance policy should be covered by the association of your complex (most of the time your monthly association dues will cover your share of this cost). However, you will be responsible for purchasing a renter's-type policy to cover the interior of your unit.

Condo Owners (Renter's / Content / HO-6) Insurance

If you are buying a condo-type property, make sure you obtain a renter's-type insurance policy (known as "HO-6" or "content insurance") to protect your personal belongings. If you have been renting, you should have had this type of insurance to protect your personal belongings. In the event of a fire, the insurance policy for the association will cover the repair of the building and any internal walls, ceilings, etc. But that policy will not cover your clothes, appliances, furniture, or any other items within your unit that are not part of the building. Take a copy of the building's policy to your agent to make sure you can pick up coverage where the building coverage leaves off.

Jewelry Policy

I have a separate policy to cover my wife's engagement ring and wedding band and a diamond ring that was passed on to me by my paternal grandfather. A typical homeowner's or renter's policy will not cover items of higher value, so you need to obtain what is known as a rider, which is an add-on to your existing policy. If our jewelry is lost or stolen, my wife and I have coverage to replace them. If we did not have this coverage, they would be very expensive to replace. (And who is not going to replace their wife's wedding rings?) Furthermore, if you do not have coverage, you are then faced with a dilemma: Do I take money from my emergency fund or retirement accounts to replace the jewelry or do I go without until we have the cash to replace them? This would be a tough choice, in my opinion, so the insurance rider is worth every penny.

Beyond a jewelry policy, your insurance agent will have coverage options for other items of higher value that are beyond what is normally covered in your policy. For example, if you have an antique car, expensive stereo equipment, or computer equipment, you want to make sure that those items are covered. So take an inventory of your possessions and let your agent know what valuables you would like covered.

Basements/Sewer Backup

As I mentioned earlier, I learned I did not have coverage for my basement in the event of a flood caused by a sewer backup, a worn-out sump pump, or a cracked wall. Whether your basement is finished or not, chances are you have items of value stored there. Possibly the most expensive items could be your laundry equipment, so you would at least want a basic policy to make sure your washer and dryer are covered. If your basement is finished, you will want a more extensive policy to cover the cost of the repair or replacement of walls, carpeting, doors, electronics, etc.

One final tip about basements: Whether your basement is finished or not, invest in plastic tubs with covers to store all of your personal items if you will not be storing them off of the floor and up on shelves. Take everything you have out of cardboard boxes. If the basement does take on water in one way or another, your stored possessions will at least be somewhat safe from water damage since the tops of these tubs are almost two feet above the ground. In addition, you will help ward off the spiders and bugs (they like cardboard).

Flood Insurance
Depending on where you live, the lender will require that you obtain flood insurance. When the title work is completed, it will be determined if your home is located in a flood plain or not. If it is, you will be required to obtain flood insurance as part of your new loan from the lender to protect the lender's interest in your home.

At the same time, you will want to double-check with your insurance agent to make certain you have coverage that will reimburse you for personal items such as furniture, electronics, etc. in the event of an unexpected flood.

Hurricane / Disaster Insurance
Depending on where you live, you are subject to hurricanes, tornados, and even earthquakes. In some cases, the lender may require that you obtain certain insurance prior to the funding of your loan, but by and large, obtaining insurance coverage for natural disasters is your responsibility. Again, check with your agent to find out exactly what your policy covers, and then obtain the necessary insurance add-ons to protect yourself in case such a disaster occurs.

Disability Insurance
Accidents do happen in which you may find yourself injured and un-

able to work. As a result, how will you bring in income to cover your bills and make your mortgage payment every month becomes a distressing concern. The result of an accident could be a temporary or permanent loss of income. As your family grows, you will find yourself with more responsibility to ensure your loved ones are taken care of if a disability prevents you from working. In truth, it does not matter if you are single or if you have a family; having disability coverage is extremely important to preserve your wealth and to allow you to still live comfortably.

Many employers offer disability insurance, for which the cost can be taken directly out of your paycheck. In other cases, you can contact an insurance agent and obtain a policy on your own. The purpose of this policy is to provide you with income if you are injured and can no longer earn an income in your current occupation. Check with your employer or insurance agent to determine coverage. The older you get and the less healthy you are, the more difficult it may be to obtain a policy. In such cases, the policy may be more expensive.

Life Insurance

Whether you are single or have a family, life insurance is a crucial part of your financial life. You do not want to leave the burden of your finances to those family members or friends left behind. Life insurance policies can be very inexpensive but, in many cases, employers do provide a basic policy at no charge or at a minimal charge, which can be taken out of your paycheck. Basically, you want to add up your financial obligations and costs for a funeral, burial, etc. and obtain a policy that will cover those costs. If you want to leave money behind for your family to be able to support themselves and make their lives easier, you should obtain a policy that has a larger payout.

Two primary types of life insurance are available: term life and whole life. Term life insurance is the simplest form in that it pays only if a death occurs during the term of the policy. A policy can be for as little as one year or as many as 30 years. Whole life insurance is a more extensive policy in that it also has an investment component and allows you to build a cash value. Whole life policies come in three variations: universal, variable, and traditional. When you are considering life insurance coverage, your insurance agent will be the best person to explain the features and benefits of whole life policies.

I personally prefer term life because it's simple, inexpensive, and the ideal coverage for somebody just starting out in life. For term life, you pay a relatively inexpensive monthly or annual fee, and you receive the appropriate insurance coverage. Since whole life has an investment component, it's more expensive. You need to look at whole life as an investment option like any other investment choice that you might consider. As your financial life grows, you may want to add variations of whole life as they may be an appropriate choice to balance out an investment portfolio. However, starting out with term life will be the best because of its simplicity and low cost.

Health Insurance

You cannot predict the medical issues you may experience throughout your life, so having health insurance is vital, especially if you are a homeowner. In my opinion, if you do not have health insurance coverage, you should not own a home. If your employer does not provide it, then find a policy on your own. If this requires you to live in a less expensive home so you can afford the insurance, then so be it. If you do not qualify for coverage, you need to find a way to get coverage. States offer coverage for people who cannot be covered on their own, and they offer coverage for children. Do whatever it takes to obtain health insurance. In fact, this is more important than owning a home. If you have to rent the rest of your life to afford health insurance, then that is ok. At least you will be able to live a better quality of life. With health insurance coverage you can maintain your health and well being without having to live in dire straits because of medical expenses.

Millions of Americans do not have health insurance coverage for themselves or for their families. If you or a family member experiences an accident or illness that requires a hospital stay or surgery, the costs of paying those medical bills could mean the difference between keeping your home and losing it. Any equity you would have gained from the down payment, paying down the principal, or appreciation may be wiped out if a hospital decides to sue you and obtains a judgment for your not paying the medical bills.

On a side note, the most common collection I see on credit reports are medical collections. This can be from a non-payment of a doctor's bill or a simple error never discovered or rectified. The reasons these collections are on the credit reports are that people ignored them, they felt insurance should have paid for it, or they just didn't have the money to pay it themselves. Many of these collections are for $500 or less, yet people did not deal with them and, thus, watched their credit scores drop. Whenever you have a medical bill, deal with it immediately. Make the necessary phone calls to ensure the bill is accurate. If it is accurate, make payment arrangements with the provider. Over the last few years, I have had various tests done to ensure I'm in good shape health-wise, but my portion of the bill after insurance paid was expensive. I contacted the hospital and/or the doctor's office and made payment arrangements. I have never had a provider say no to making that type of arrangement. They have never charged me interest on the balance, and they let me take up to a year to pay it off in full.

Starting Your Own Investment Plan

I've already emphasized many times that you need to save and invest for retirement in combination with owning a home. But the question that so many clients ask is, "How do I invest"? My answer is always the same: I can't give you specific investment advice, but I can tell you that you need a balance of investments to create safety and some level of liquidity. (Liquidity means that you have access to the money if need be.) I advise my clients to:

- Have an emergency account
- Contribute to a 401(k) or 403(b)
- Contribute to a personal investment plan.

Maintaining an Emergency Account

When you become a homeowner, it's never a good idea to live paycheck to paycheck without having emergency money set aside. You need to have money that you can easily access in the event of a big emergency such as a house repair, insurance deductibles, or a medical emergency. The rule of thumb is that you should have on hand at least six months' worth of expenses in savings (although many experts say eight to ten months, if not a full year). For instance, if your expenses run $4,000 per month, you should have $24,000 sitting in cash in the bank.

I realize that this can be a lot of money for some people. But you can start your emergency fund small by keeping one month's worth of expenses aside and then work yourself up to two months' and so on. Try to balance what you are spending every month with what you are putting into retirement accounts and into emergency savings. Saving is hard to do in our consumeristic society, but when you are about to buy something, always ask yourself the question, Do I really need that? Then take the money you would have spent on that item and put it into your emergency account. Think of it as buying yourself interest that the bank will pay you.

You will also want to set up a separate savings account for your emergency fund, and then do your best to pretend the money is not there. You should also set up an auto transfer from your checking account to your emergency fund account to move funds on the day after you get paid. This will help prevent you from falling into the bad habit of thinking that you can use that money for something this month and then pick up again with your savings program the next month. It never happens! You need to be committed and diligent in this area. And even while money sitting in a low-interest savings account is not always profitable, money invested in retirement accounts is not easily accessible in an emergency. When it is accessible, it will cost you quite a bit in fees and/or tax penalties to withdraw. The point is to make sure that your emergency fund money is within reach should something come up for which you need immediate access to those funds.

As stated earlier, by starting out in a condominium- or townhouse-type of home, you are reducing the possibility of unexpected expenses. Since you are paying association dues that take care of the exterior parts of the building, you are left to worry only about the things that can go wrong within your unit. Problems within your unit will often be less expensive to repair than exterior ones. If you bought your home with a home warranty, then you have the insurance to cover expenses if any of the mechanicals malfunction within your unit. Thinking and preparing like this will make the purchase of your new home a bit easier.

Contributing to a 401(k) or 403(b)

Many employers offer retirement plans through 401(k) or 403(b). 401(k)s are for employees working for a business, while 403(b)s are for non-profit organizations or employees working for the state, such as teachers. The basic concept of these investment options is that the money is taken from your paycheck before tax. You will then pay taxes on the money when you draw from the account after retirement.

In some cases employers will match your contribution to these accounts. For example, if you contribute 3% of your gross pay to your 401(k), your employer might match up to 100% of that contribution. If you then put 4% of your pay into the 401(k), the employer will still only match the 3%. Every employer will have different guidelines as to how their retirement plans work. If your employer matches in any way, this is essentially free money. Most investment advisors I know recommend contributing as much as the employer is matching if you can afford it.

If you ever need money, the downside to taking money from your 401(k) or 403(b), if you can, is that you might be heavily penalized and taxed. This is why I always tell people not to keep all their eggs in one basket. Instead, they need to set up a personal investment plan.

Contributing to a Personal Investment Plan

Aside from having an emergency fund and contributing to your employer's retirement plan, you should have a well-balanced personal investment plan. To do this, you will need the help of a financial advisor. The sooner you have a financial advisor working on your behalf, the odds are that your investments will perform better over time. There are a variety of investment advisors out there, so it's your job to find a reputable one. My advice would be to talk with elders who have done well with a very balanced investment plan and find out who their advisor is. You can also seek out Barron's magazine, which rates the top advisors by state. There is nothing wrong with contacting them and working with the best.

The reason you want to have a personal investment plan is that if you ever need access to money, you can easily do so by selling a portion of your investment. So rather than paying a penalty and tax on the entire withdrawal from your employer-sponsored plan, you are only paying tax on the gain your investment has made since you contributed money to this investment after income tax from your paycheck rather than before tax in your employer-sponsored plan.

The one final piece I can share with you is to educate yourself about investing by reading some books. If you understand the basic concepts of investing, you will feel so much more comfortable about it and therefore feel much more comfortable when listening to the advice an investment advisor is sharing with you. I have found that any book written by Ric Edelman is easy to read as he really does a great job of explaining a complicated subject. Suze Orman also has some great investment books written for women.

Types of Financial Advisors

There are two types of advisors in the marketplace: fee-based and transaction-based. I've included short descriptions of each type, but ultimately, as I mentioned earlier in this book, you would want a fee-based advisor.

Transaction-Based Advisors
Transaction-based advisors will charge you for every transaction

they make on your behalf. For example, every time a stock is sold, the advisor makes money. Therefore, the more transactions they make, the more money they make. If an advisor makes 100 stock trades for you at $10 per trade, this advisor just made $1,000. Who knows if those stock trades gained or lost in value for your portfolio? As you can well imagine, this type of advisor is not necessarily operating in your best interest. In certain situations, it would be better to use a transaction-based advisor, such as when you are older, you are using very conservative investments, or you are completing very few transactions during the year. When you are first starting out, your primary goal usually will be to grow the value of your portfolio witch may include many transactions, which is why the fee-based advisor would be more appropriate.

Fee-Based Advisors

Fee-based advisors earn their income as a fixed percentage of your portfolio's value on an annual basis. As your portfolio grows, their income grows. Say the fee is 2% of your portfolio's value. If your portfolio's value is $100,000, they would earn $2,000. If they grow your portfolio's value to $400,000, (regardless of the number of transactions they do), the advisor would earn $8,000. If an advisor grew my portfolio from $100,000 to $400,000, I would gladly pay him or her the $8,000 as they have certainly earned it. If the value of your portfolio declines, so would their earnings. This situation is win/win, which is why this type of advisor is preferred.

Keeping Good Records

When I bought my home, I appreciated the fact that the previous owner had saved all of the owner's manuals for the various appliances, fixtures, smoke alarms, etc. that were purchased for the home. What made it even better was that the dates of the purchases were marked on the manuals. This is very helpful to you as a homeowner because things are bound to break, so having on hand the right information regarding the various appliances, etc. will help make repairs easier to deal with. I have also bought homes for which I did not receive any documentation about anything within the home, which made it very difficult to figure out model numbers and obtain replacement parts. My advice is to start a file and any time you buy something that will become a permanent part of the home, file the owner's manuals and mark the dates of purchases on them. Make a copy of the receipt and staple it to the manual. You never know when you will need that information in the future.

Another good record-keeping tip is to keep a photographic inventory of higher-priced items. For example, if you bought a new couch or an expensive flat-panel TV, take pictures of those items, make copies of the receipts, and file them away someplace safe. In addition, keep a separate copy of all important papers in a safety deposit box at your local bank. In the event of fire, flood, burglary, or some other mishap, your papers will be protected and will be proof of ownership of the items and of how much you paid for them. Should the original documentation be destroyed along with your possessions, these papers will be necessary. You can buy software programs that will help you keep track and create an inventory of your items. Just do a search online for "home inventory." You can also videotape all the rooms in your house and then put a copy of that tape in your safety deposit box for future reference.

A deposit box is an ideal place to keep important papers such as the new deed to your home, birth certificates, marriage certificates, passports, and any other legal documents. Other items you can store include jewelry that you don't wear very often, computer data backups, and other valuables. Various sizes of boxes are available and are usually offered for a very reasonable cost. In some cases, the bank may provide you with a box at no charge, depending on the type of banking accounts you have with them.

CHAPTER 11
Refinancing

After purchasing a home, you will want or need to refinance your mortgage at some point, so I decided to include a chapter about refinancing so you become familiar with the concept.   There are many positive reasons to refinance along with some bad ones, as I will point out in this chapter. So, let me share with you the five main reasons that you should refinance your home:

- Debt consolidation
- Home improvement
- Lowering interest rate
- New or changing loan programs
- Divorce

Debt Consolidation

Unfortunately, people often find themselves in a position in which they have to use equity in their home to consolidate debt to improve their cash flow. This could be a result of mismanagement of money by overspending, unexpected loss of income from job loss, or unexpected medical bills. Whatever the case may be, using the equity in your home is one method of reducing some of the stress you are experiencing with high bills and turning the situation into a positive by consolidating the debt into a single new loan. As a result, you will lower your monthly outlay of cash. You can also convert non-tax-deductible debt to tax-deductible debt, considering that interest paid on a mortgage is tax-deductible while interest paid on credit cards and car payments is not. Let me caution you to not use the equity you gain in your home as a cash machine because you are living beyond your means. You will never create wealth or have your home paid off if you live beyond your means.

One couple came to see me because they needed to consolidate some credit card debt. *Figure 11-1* is an analysis of their situation:

Debt Consolidation Analysis

Debt Type	Lender	Rate	Balance	Payment	Tax Ded.
Mortgage	1st Mortgage	6.25%	$207,772	$1,305	$303
Mortgage	2nd Mortgage	8.25%	$27,696	$291	$53
Credit Card	Mastercard	9.50%	$12,486	$456	$0
Credit Card	Visa	19.99%	$8,700	$169	$0
Credit Card	Discover	19.99%	$5,873	$104	$0
Totals		12.8% avg	$262,526	$2,325	$356

Below is a new mortgage that consolidated all of the above debt into a single new loan that provided for a single monthly payment.

New Loan	Term	Rate	New Balance	Payment	Tax Ded.
30-Year Fixed	360 months	6.75%	$266,000	$1,725	$419

By refinancing their debt, they improved their monthly cash flow by $600, reducing their payments from $2,325 to $1,725. They also increased their monthly tax deductions by $63 from converting non-tax-deductible debt (the credit cards) to tax-deductible debt.

Figure 11-1

As you can see in this scenario, this couple's cash flow was limited because of the amount of money going out every month. In addition, their average household interest rate for debt was 12.8%.

Let's take a look at how their cash flow would perform by consolidating all of their debt into a single new mortgage loan. After consolidating their debt, their interest rate was higher on their mortgage. The higher rate is primarily a result of a lower credit score from having high credit card balances combined with the current market conditions for interest rates. However, as you can see, the interest rate is irrelevant considering the savings the couple is achieving on a monthly basis. So, focusing on the interest rate is not always important. In this case, they lowered their overall household interest rate by 6.05%.

Now let's take a look at the savings this couple has now achieved. You will see that they are saving $600 per month in cash flow. They also have converted their non-preferred debt (credit cards, auto loans, medical bills) to preferred debt (tax-deductible) and have increased their tax benefit by $63 per month. They have improved their financial standing by an amazing $7,956 over a year's period. Remember: Uncle Sam allows you to deduct your mortgage interest on your tax return. Now that this couple has taken out a new, larger loan, they will be paying more in interest (because the money paid on credit cards is not tax-deductible), thus increasing the amount of their tax benefit and the amount for which they will be credited on their tax return. *Figure 11-2* summarizes these savings.

Savings Summary by Consolidating Debt			
Monthly Payment/Cash Flow		**Monthly Tax Benefits**	
Payment before	$2,325	Tax benefits before	$356
Payment after –	$1,725	Tax benefits after –	$419
Payment savings =	**$600**	**Tax benefits gained =**	**$63**
Annualized savings	$7,200	Annualized gain	$756

Figure 11-2

If you have equity in your home to use to consolidate your debt, the savings achieved from doing so can be significant to turning your situation around if you are in a tough financial position.

After a meeting with me, the couple in the previous example could see the light at the end of the tunnel for their future. They committed to taking 50% of their monthly savings and using it to pay extra on their mortgage every month. It's important to know that you don't want to divert all of your money to paying down your mortgage balance. You still want to fund your savings and retirement accounts so you have cash available for emergencies. In the next chapter, I will share some methods of paying down your mortgage.

To have their mortgage paid off in 19.9 years, this couple will have to be disciplined and change their spending habits so they do not find themselves with credit card debt again:

Extra monthly payment toward principal:	**$300**
Mortgage will be paid off early in:	**19.9 Years**
Money saved by paying less in interest cost:	**$136,402**

This couple is now confident they will be able to remain focused on the future rather than on today. Ideally, they would take a portion of the savings and allocate that toward an investment account so they can take advantage of the power of compounding interest to save for retirement.

In summary, consolidating your debt can help you to improve your cash flow and convert your non-preferred debt to preferred debt. This is the point at which you want to change your bad habits to avoid getting into the same situation again.

Home Improvement

A source of money to improve your home can come from your home's equity. You can obtain this money from either taking out a home equity loan or from refinancing your entire loan for a higher amount than you owe and taking cash out. The current market and your credit scores will determine which road you take.

I talked about home equity loans previously in this book. Basically, a home equity loan is a second loan on your home. Sometimes people who have been in their home a long time have a lot of equity and will want to spend some of the equity to update their home. A second loan is a viable option if you are going to be able to pay it back within a three- to five-year period.

Interest rates on home equity loans are tied to the Prime Rate, which is published in daily newspapers. The Prime Rate changes as our economy changes over time. For example, at the time of this writing, the Prime Rate had just been lowered to 3.25%, so obtaining a home equity loan around 3.24% to 4% was highly possible. Keep in mind that if the Prime Rate goes up, your rate will go up as well, thus increasing your payment. You could obtain a fixed-rate home equity line, but those are typically at a higher interest rate. If home equity rates are lower than traditional fixed-rate mortgages, then taking out a home equity line is a smart decision. However, as soon as home equity rates climb to be compatible with long-term rates, you will want to convert that home equity line into a single new loan on your home.

If home equity rates are, say, 8% and long-term mortgage money is only 6.5%, you would want to take out one new loan rather than a home equity loan so the cost of your borrowed money is less.

When the time comes for you to explore those options, you should sit down and discuss with a mortgage professional such things as the terms of current interest rates, the time you need to pay back the amount you intend to borrow, and the amount you need. A mortgage professional will have the tools necessary to run the calculations to determine if a home equity loan or a new single loan would be best.

Home improvements can be a good reason to refinance, as you are increasing the value of your home. There is no better place to get a loan than from your own home, considering the interest on the loan is tax-deductible. This can be a more affordable way to fund improvements than using high-interest rate credit cards or taking money from retirement accounts.

Lowering Interest Rate

Having a good relationship with your mortgage professional will come in handy when you want to refinance to obtain a lower interest rate. Your mortgage professional will help you figure out the best path to take. As I mentioned earlier, interest rates can and do change daily, so taking advantage of dips in the market so you can get a lower interest rate (thus lowering your monthly payment) can be helpful in improving cash flow. It will also help you pay down your home faster, which I will talk about in the next chapter.

Let's just say you obtained a $200,000 loan at 6.25% interest on a 30-year fixed, resulting in a payment of $1,231 per month. Roughly seven months after you closed on your home, the market changed, and now interest rates are 5.75% on a 30-year fixed. By refinancing your mortgage, you can achieve a new payment of $1,167 per month, providing you a savings of $64 per month. If you are working with a good mortgage professional, you will complete the refinance at no cost to you, and therefore you would realize the benefit of the $64 savings immediately. That $64 would add up to $3,840 after five years.

You could take that $64 and put it back toward your mortgage or you could invest it. If you put it back toward your mortgage, you could pay your home off 3.5 years earlier, saving you $29,019 in interest. If you invested it at a very conservative 3% interest rate, that $64 could grow to $37,789 over the next 30 years. (Recall the compound interest formula I previously talked about in Chapter 2.)

You may not be able to obtain a no-cost refinance, or you may have to complete a limited cost refinance. In either case, let's just say the closing costs would be $2,000. By dividing the $2,000 by the $64 monthly savings from the previous example, it would take you 31 months to realize the financial benefit of the refinance. This is when you have to consider how long you will be living in the home and the longer term impact of the savings.

For example, if you knew you were going to be living in the home for another 10 years, by refinancing and paying the $2,000 in costs, you would save $5,696 over that 10-year period.

To place them in better positions, I have refinanced clients countless times as interest rates fell. In December 2008, long-term interest rates fell to their lowest in years, creating a refinance boom that many of my existing and new clients were able to take advantage of and save. When you are working with a mortgage professional who closely monitors your mortgage for you, you will be able to reap the benefits of these opportunities. A good mortgage professional will notify you when these changes are happening rather than your having to figure it out on your own haphazardly, via the news or through conversations with friends.

Let's say you have had your mortgage for five years and an opportunity came up to save by lowering your interest rate. One concern many have had in the past is they did not want to stretch their new mortgage back out to 30 years. In such cases, we amortized their new loan over 25 years, which allowed them to stay on target for the payoff of their mortgage.

In *Figure 11-3* , I demonstrate how the lower interest rate affects the borrower's payment if they have had their first loan for five years. As you can see, if they refinanced their loan into a new 30-year fixed rate loan, the payment would be significantly less compared to that of a new, refinanced 25-year loan. However, the 25-year loan would result in a smaller payment amount compared to that of their existing loan and would keep their payoff date (25 years from now) the same.

Refinancing With Lower Rate / Term Analysis					
	Balance	**Rate**	**Payment**	**Term**	**Time Left**
Original Loan	$250K	6%	$1,499	30 years	25 years
New Loan 30 Yrs	$220K	5.75%	$1,284	30 years	30 years
New Loan 25 Yrs	$220K	5.75%	$1,384	25 years	25 years

The 25-year term keeps the borrower on track with their original payoff date.

Figure 11-3

New or Changing Loan Programs

Other reasons people refinance are that their loan program is changing or a loan program that is more attractive and beneficial to their situation becomes available.

For instance, if you have an ARM that is coming due and you are reaching the 5-year mark, you may want to refinance since once your ARM adjusts, your payment will increase. If you know your loan program is going to be expiring within the next 12 months, tell your mortgage professional. He/she should be tuned into your situation to alert you to market conditions that will allow you to take advantage of lower interest rates. By planning ahead, you will be able to take advantage of the market swing. If you wait until your ARM expires, you will run the risk of a higher rate. In addition, by letting your ARM expire, you will be forced to make a higher payment because of the rate adjustment.

Sometimes lenders introduce new loan programs that did not exist when you took your loan out. Your mortgage professional should inform you of new loan programs that will benefit you in the form of lower monthly payments or the security of a longer term fixed rate.

Another time to refinance as a result of changing loan programs is when you put less than 20% down and are paying mortgage insurance. Since your home over time is going to appreciate in value, your loan-to-value (LTV) (loan balance / value of home = LTV) will decrease. If you had put 10% down and over time your home's value had risen while your loan balance had gone down as a result of your monthly payments, you would therefore have appreciated into a lower loan-to-value ratio, as I point out in Figure *11-4*. If you remember from my earlier discussions in this book, the mortgage insurance falls off at 78% automatically, but at 80% you can pick up the phone and call your lender to have the mortgage insurance removed.

Refinancing by Changing Loan Programs	
Original Loan	**After 4 Years**
Home Value $200,000 10% Down Payment – $20,000 Loan Balance =$180,000 **Loan to Value Ratio** **90%** ($180,000 / $200,000) = LTV	New Home Value $225,101 Loan Balance $171,110 **Loan to Value Ratio** **76%** ($171,110 / $225,101) = LTV

Figure 11-4

In *Figure 11-4*, your loan-to-value was reduced from 90% to 76%. As a result, more attractive loan programs may exist with better interest rates that may benefit you since you are in an LTV position of less than 80%. You will want to consider the costs and your future to determine if refinancing makes sense.

This is another reason that you want to have a solid working relationship with a mortgage professional. After a period of time, you can pick up the phone and call your mortgage professional to discuss your situation if you know your home's value has risen. To find out if the value of your home has risen, you can find out what similar models of homes are selling for in the current market or have an independent appraisal completed.

Divorce

If you know that you are going to get divorced, the only way to remove your spouse from the responsibility of the loan is to refinance. If the two parties involved mutually decide that one spouse is going to keep the home after the divorce, then the refinancing needs to take place early on in the divorce process. In this way, both parties can be assured that the division of property will be clear-cut and without incident.

Unfortunately, there have been many cases in which the couple divorcing has let things get nasty. The result was that they ended up ruining each other's credit and therefore making the process of refinancing next to impossible if their original intent was to let one spouse live in the home so the children could attend the same school. If you ruin each other's credit, it will take you years to repair the damage. My advice is to meet early on with a mortgage professional along with your respective attorneys to decide how to deal with the home. I can't tell you how many times I have seen such a situation go bad; the divorcing couple is forced to sell the home while watching all of their equity evaporate to pay attorney fees.

Since 50% of all married couples in the United States get divorced, it would be careless of me to not comment on this area as this is a big killer of wealth creation with homeownership.

Mortgage Management

Many good quality mortgage professionals across the country offer a mortgage management program, including me. All of my clients are placed into my mortgage management program at no charge to them. As a result, my clients save thousands of dollars over time.

The purposes of a mortgage management program are to:
- Minimize the cost of your money borrowed from lower interest rates.
- Minimize the cost of your loan as loan programs change.
- Provide ongoing education on matters related to real estate and your home.
- Conduct annual reviews to see if any changes are necessary based on interest rates, appreciation, investment opportunities, and/or tax maximization.

When enrolled in such a program, you won't need to worry about your mortgage once you close on the purchase of your home. If interest rates drop or loan programs that will lower your payment and improve your cash flow change, you will be alerted to the opportunity by the mortgage professional you are working with.

The disadvantage to not having your mortgage managed by a professional is that you are assuredly missing countless opportunities to save when market conditions change. You hear from friends, co-workers, or the news that rates have dropped, but then you find out that you did not act fast enough to take advantage of the opportunity because you were not alerted to that fact ahead of time. Work with a professional who has a mortgage management program. You will ultimately save thousands of dollars over the course of owning your home.

Earlier in this book, I provided you with various resources to find a good quality mortgage professional. The one point I can't emphasize enough is that you must work with a professional who has your long-term interests at heart. Stay away from those who are looking at you as a mere one-time transaction—and there are many of them out there who would do so.

CHAPTER 12
Your Mortgage Strategy

In closing this book, I want to talk a bit about the strategy you should have in place for managing your mortgage. The creation of wealth from owning a home is dependent on how you choose to manage your mortgage during the course of owning your home.

In many cases, a mortgage is no longer viewed as a debt; it is seen more as an asset that is part of the financial tools available to you to help create wealth. As I talked about earlier, since the Great Depression, banks can no longer demand your loan be due with a 30-day notice. Today, all the bank can do is require that you make your payment on a monthly basis. The bank has to honor the terms of your loan until the end. However, you have the choice to pay the loan off early if you so choose.

So, let me ask you: How would you feel if you were in a good position financially to pay off your mortgage when you wanted to or had a plan to have your mortgage paid off by a certain date?

The point in time when your assets exceed your debts and you are in a position to pay off the mortgage (as I previously mentioned in the Introduction) is commonly known as your freedom point. In high school or college, you probably learned a basic accounting formula known as:

Assets − Liabilities = Net Worth

I talked about net worth previously as I showed how net worth is created as a result of homeownership and your savings. When your assets exceed your liabilities, you earn a certain financial freedom at which point you have flexibility and opportunity. You have the flexibility financially to invest in certain opportunities that you would not have had before. For example, you could invest in a business, you could buy a second home, you could buy an investment property, or you could invest in the stock market—the opportunities are abundant. You can do many things when you have financial freedom.

I believe all of us want to reach our freedom point sooner or later, but the sooner you reach your freedom point, the better off you will be. For this reason alone, you do not want to own a home that is beyond your means or have a mortgage that takes up too much of your monthly income. Do you really need the biggest house on the block? What about living in a more modest home whereby you can continue to pay your mortgage and invest for retirement? The bigger the house payment is, the longer it will take you to become financially free. By having a plan, controlling your liabilities (expenses/costs), and watching your assets grow, your freedom point will arrive sooner than you think.

Treat Your Mortgage Differently

Depending on your financial accomplishments in life, you will treat your mortgage differently than others may. For some people, having the mortgage paid off is important. For others, keeping the mortgage to utilize as a tax benefit to offset income from other investments is of more importance. Each person is different in how they choose to manage their mortgage. Ultimately, you have to do what you are most comfortable with. The purpose of this chapter is to shed light on strategies and concepts that you can take advantage of to reach your freedom point faster. There are no quick schemes in achieving financial freedom. The concept is simple in that you either have to pay your debts down faster or increase your income and savings faster. Each person will have a balance of debt reduction and income/savings management in their life. People who find themselves in trouble and in foreclosure were often poor money managers to begin with and found that their debt was growing while their income/savings was decreasing or remaining flat. This is a recipe for disaster. So it all comes back to not overbuying on your first home. Your first home will be the biggest payment you are responsible for every month. Keeping that payment at a reasonable, comfortable amount will allow you to work on raising the income/savings portion of the formula.

The "Wheel of Impact"

Considering your home is both your largest liability and potentially your largest asset, let's first take a look at all the areas of your financial life impacted by your mortgage. The choice of the type of home and mortgage affects all the areas shown in the outer circles of the illustration in *Figure 12-1* that I created, known as the "Wheel of Impact":

Wheel of Impact ©Douglas Boncosky

Figure 12-1

Unfortunately, I have found in my practice that people do not take all the areas in the outer circles into consideration or they end up working with a mortgage professional who either does not know about or talk about most of these areas when discussing mortgage programs. Therefore, I want to help you gain an understanding of these areas as they are central to managing your mortgage.

The Center Circle—Your Home / Mortgage

Choosing a home and mortgage is an extremely important decision to make. Your choice ultimately affects all the areas of the circle, which I will explain.

Down Payment

The amount of money you have to put down dictates the type of loan program you end up using. The more money you have to put down, the less the cost will be to borrow the money you need to purchase your home. The flipside is that the more you put down, the less cash you have available in your savings for emergencies or investment opportunities.

As a first-time homebuyer, your goal should be to put as little down as allowed (unless you have a family member who is going to gift you a sizeable down payment). Even if you have enough money for a 10% down payment, you should put less down. Having liquidity is essential; if you lost your job or had some sort of demand for cash, you would have money readily available to you. If all your money is tied up in equity in your home and you lose your job, you will not be able to refinance to take the equity out to cover the demand for cash.

One of the bigger questions that a first-time homebuyer has is, "How much money should I use for a down payment?" As a first-time homebuyer, you should put as little down as possible so that you can preserve your cash for emergencies.

In *Figure 12-2*, I analyze Henry Homebuyer, who earns $75,000 per year and is therefore in the 25% tax bracket. He has worked hard and saved

$35,000. He will be buying a $150,000 home. I will compare the choice of putting down 20% in Scenario 1 to 3.5% in Scenario 2.

In *Figure 12-2*, my preferred method for advising a client would be Scenario 2. As you can see, the net worth after five years in Scenario 1 is greater than that of Scenario 2. You might say, "Wait a minute, I thought the title of this book is Create Wealth with Homeownership? . . . I'm going with Scenario 1!" Well, let me explain why Scenario 2 is the better option.

My reason for advising Henry Homebuyer to use Scenario 2 is liquidity. In Scenario 1, he would have used the majority of his savings for a down payment. So, in the event he had a job loss, major medical expense, or some other situation that required money, he would have been left with very little, if any, after the expense. If he lost his job, he may only be able to sustain his housing payment for six months after he factors in the taxes, insurance, and HOA dues. After six months, Henry falls behind, he can't access his equity because he does not have a job, and once he loses his home to foreclosure, he will lose all of the down payment money he put into the home, leaving him penniless. Henry would be in dire straits in this case.

In Scenario 2, Henry could continue to make his mortgage payment for roughly 19 months if he lost his job. This would allow him plenty of time to find another job and get back on his feet. Although not ideal, in this scenario, Henry could sleep better at night knowing that he has some time to weather this storm.

After five years, Henry has more in investments than in equity in Scenario 2, which is the situation you would want to be in. You do not want to have more of your wealth in the equity of your home than you do in savings and investments. My reason is simple: you can't access the equity if you do not have a job. If you're in the later years of your life and you have a few hundred thousand in savings and investments, then your equity position is not necessarily an issue, but keep in mind that the strategy you have in place regarding your investments and equity management will be

How Much You Should Put Down on a Home?

Scenario 1 (Big Down Payment)	Scenario 2 (Small Down Payment)
30-Year Fixed-Rate Mortgage 5.75% APR (interest rate) $30,000 Down Payment $0 left to invest $0 upfront Mortgage Insurance $120,000 Loan Amount (80% LTV)	30-Year Fixed-Rate Mortgage 6.00% APR (interest rate) $5,250 Down Payment (3.5% FHA) $24,750 left to invest $2,533 FHA Upfront Mortgage Insurance $147,283 Loan Amount (98%)
Payment & Taxes $700 Monthly Payment $0 Monthly Mortgage Insurance $700 Gross Monthly Payment	**Payment & Taxes** $883 Monthly Payment $68 Monthly Mortgage Insurance $951 Gross Monthly Payment
Tax Benefits* $110 Tax Benefit $590 After-Tax Mortgage Payment	**Tax Benefits*** $133 Tax Benefit $818 After-Tax Mortgage Payment

Investment / Savings Analysis
$5,000 left in savings
Sends $328 to investments
    every month
4% Rate of Return
	Investment / Savings Analysis
	$29,750 left in savings
	Sends $100 to investments
	    every month
	4% Rate of Return

After 5 Years (typical time a first-time homebuyer is in their first home)

$165,612 Home Value
    (2% appreciation)
$27,854 Investment Value
$54,298 Equity Position
	$165,612 Home Value
	    (2% appreciation)
	$42,955 Investment Value
	$28,559 Equity Position

$82,152 Net Worth	**$71,554 Net Worth**

*Tax benefits are calculated by averaging the savings over the life of the loan. Actual savings during the first five years would be greater since more of your monthly mortgage payment goes toward interest than in the later years of your mortgage. I prefer to use averages when I am calculating scenarios.

Figure 12-2

far different from what it would be when you are first starting out.

You will also note that Henry's cost of money is higher in Scenario 2 since he has a higher interest rate and has to pay mortgage insurance. The higher cost of money is ok because he has liquidity. Sometimes peace of mind costs more, but it's worth it.

Also, you will notice that after five years, Henry's loan-to-value has changed from 98% to 83%. He could wait another year or two while his home appreciated into an 80% LTV position to remove mortgage insurance or simply refinance and bring $4,112 to the table to reach the 80% LTV position, thus lowering his cost of money. If he did come to the table with $4,112, he could afford it since he has accumulated $42,955 in savings and investments.

For these reasons, I advocate putting as little down as possible when buying your first home. As time is on your side, your home is appreciating, you are saving and investing even more, and your strategy can and most likely will change to accommodate your changing financial situation.

Earlier in the book I mentioned to be careful of heeding everything your parents and grandparents have to say. Their strategies and views on money will be quite different because of where they are at in their life and because times have changed since they bought their homes. However, if your parents or grandparents are helping you with a gift to be used for a down payment, your strategy for your new loan will be different.

As I have repeatedly stated in this book, as long as you are able to have money set aside for emergencies and you continue to save and invest for retirement, your choice for a down payment will fall in line with how much money you have saved and are comfortable parting with.

Every situation is going to be different, so my advice is not to use the examples in this book as your own, but to sit down with a mortgage professional who understands these concepts and can then work with you to develop a strategy for buying your first home.

Monthly Payment and Cash Flow

The loan program you have also impacts your cash flow. This is a huge factor because as a first-time homebuyer, you may be younger or just starting out in your career and not earning as much right now as you will in the future (as your career conceivably grows). Therefore, you may only be able to qualify for certain loan programs. So what you really want to consider in this situation is the different types of loan programs that will allow for the lowest monthly payment, not to mention the lowest down payment.

Pay Off Date

At some point, you will want to have your mortgage paid off. Some people want to keep the loan the full 30 years or whatever amortization term they have decided upon, while others prefer to get the home paid off as soon as possible. The loan program you choose can either accelerate the pay off or slow it down. Some programs will help you pay the loan off faster, while for others you can pay interest only on a 30-year loan without ever paying the balance down. This in the end is determined by your investment and retirement objectives. Those working with a financial advisor will be more apt to keep the mortgage because of the tax benefits to offset other investments, while those managing their own retirement goals will more than likely simply want to be rid of the mortgage debt as soon as possible.

Emergency Fund / Savings

You should always maintain an emergency fund, so the question is: Do you want to use all of your money for the down payment, or put less down and accept a higher monthly payment on your mortgage? Experts suggest you should have at least eight to ten months' worth of expenses in an emergency fund set aside. I would elect to put less down to maintain an emergency fund so that I could pay for unexpected expenses. You do not want to have more equity in your home than you do cash for emergencies and money in your investment accounts. Remember that you are not able to access the equity for cash if you lose your job or your credit score gets worse.

Tax Benefits

As the IRS Tax Code states, mortgage interest and property taxes are tax-deductible. At the time of this writing, mortgage insurance was tax-deductible as well. Depending on your investment philosophy, you may want to maximize your tax deductions by having an interest-only loan. Furthermore, if you have mortgage insurance and make over $100,000, you may want a lender-paid mortgage insurance-type loan. The mortgage insurance is not deductible if you earn greater than $100,000, but the interest on a lender-paid plan is deductible. As I discussed earlier in this book, as a first-time homebuyer, you will find that receiving the tax benefits for mortgage interest and property taxes will make a significant difference in your cash flow over renting.

Equity Position

The equity position you have in your home is the difference between the value of the home and what you owe on it. For example, if your home is worth $200,000 and you owe $150,000, your equity position is $50,000. This is also known as your loan-to-value ratio, which, using this example, would be 75%. Depending on your loan-to-value ratio, your interest rate will vary, thus making the cost of money borrowed higher or lower. Some prefer to maintain minimal equity in their home and keep the value separate in a relatively safe investment that grows. Others prefer to build the equity by paying down their mortgage quicker or just staying under 80% loan-to-value to ensure they qualify for the best interest rates. Again, you do not want to have more equity in your home than you do in cash and investments.

Appreciation

Appreciation is the most important component in helping you create wealth with your home. Real estate does appreciate over time. Unfortunately, the appreciation does not happen equally year after year nor does it move equally in our local towns and villages. In some years appreciation could be growing in double digits while in other years it could very well be zero or even negative. When looking to buy a home, be sure you are looking at historical data so you can make an educated decision to buy in an area where homes have been appreciating over time. Avoid buying in areas that are prone to major economic impacts from company closings, crime, etc. Appreciation will allow you to move into a bigger home more easily, since you can transfer that equity into a down payment on a new home.

Long-Term Strategy

The mortgage you take out today does impact your future plans. Knowing what financial moves you might make in the future will help you decide how you manage the current mortgage you have. Planning for future upgrades in your home as your income increases is important. Knowing how to navigate the mortgage maze to make loan programs work to your favor is also a helpful part of your strategy. Now, when purchasing your first home, your strategy is to get into the home, but you must accept that your strategy is going to change over time.

Quality of Life and Your Lifestyle

A home is more than an investment; it is shelter for you and your family. So naturally, where you want to live and the type of home you choose to buy are important factors in maintaining a high quality of life. Your home is a reflection of who you are and often times the people who you want to associate with. Schools for your children, shopping areas, churches, and so many other elements influence your choice for buying a home in a particular location. The downside to buying a home purely as a lifestyle choice is that people can find themselves leaning toward purchasing a home that might be a bit beyond their means because they are trying to appear as if they have more money than they do. If you make this choice, it will hurt your cash flow. This ultimately affects your quality of life negatively if you have to eat mac and cheese for dinner every night. I'm sure you have heard the phrase "house rich, cash poor." Avoid owning the big, empty house with no cash flow and opt to purchase a home that allows you to live comfortably and still contribute to savings and retirement accounts.

Investment Plan

In addition to having an emergency fund, you should be funding retirement accounts. You can create a great deal of net worth over 30 years of homeownership, but that net worth is not liquid since you can't touch it unless you sell the home or take out a new loan against the value of the home. So, as part of creating wealth, you want to have an investment plan for your retirement as I talked about in Chapter 10. Your plan can include your 401(k)/403(b) contribution from your employer, your own retirement accounts, or a combination of both. A good financial advisor will help you develop a solid financial plan to prepare for retirement. The sooner you begin working with a reliable advisor, the better off you will be.

That is the Wheel of Impact. As you can see, many parts of your life are affected by your homebuying and loan program choices. Having an understanding of this when you sit down with a mortgage professional will help you clearly identify what areas are most important for you at that time in your life. You can then discuss loan solutions and develop a mortgage strategy that will most successfully suit your needs.

Figure 12-3 shows how having more cash than equity contributes to a healthy financial situation:

As you can see from *Figure 12-3*, a "Good" situation to be in is one where you have a balance of cash, investments, and equity in your home. The two "Bad" situations are those in which people are in an unbalanced position and, because of the credit card debt, are unable to properly fund savings and investments. Furthermore, in situation two, you can see that most of their wealth is tied up in equity in their home, so as soon as they have a job loss or medical emergency, they may not be in a position to access the equity for cash.

Accelerating the Creation of Wealth

As I mentioned at the start of this chapter, you need to have a mortgage plan. A part of this plan is accelerating the creation of wealth by making some small changes to your cash flow. When you take out a new mortgage, you have to look at that mortgage over time in addition to the short-term. For example, when you open an investment account, you are typically ad-

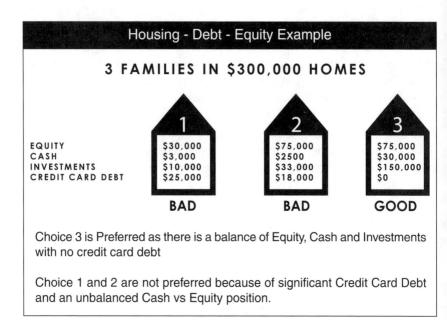

Figure 12-3

vised to look at the performance of that account over 30-40 years until you will need to withdraw from it at retirement. Along the way you will make some adjustments, but by and large you are generally advised to leave the investment intact while spreading your risk among different types of investments. If any one investment is performing poorly, the other investments will pick up the slack.

With homeownership, you need to look at the long-term picture regarding where you want to be when you retire. If you buy your first home at age 28 and want to retire and have the home paid off by age 65, that leaves you only 37 years from now to accomplish this goal. Assuming you take out a 30-year mortgage and stay in the same home for the next 30 years, you will have the home paid off seven years early. The likelihood of your staying in your first home for 30 years is very remote though. When considering statistics from the US Census Bureau and the National Association of Realtors, you will more than like move three to four times over your lifetime and complete another five to eight refinance transactions along the way.

You can accelerate the creation of wealth by either paying off your home early or maintaining your mortgage to accelerate your investments so that you will accumulate the funds to pay off your home when you want to.

Paying Off Your Home

Reaching your freedom point can make a huge difference in how you create wealth over time. Paying off your home or being in a position to pay off your home has a huge impact on your cash flow and quality of life. Here is what you could do if you did not have a mortgage on your primary home:

- Have more cash flow once the mortgage is paid off
- Buy a second home or investment property
- Pay for your child's college education
- Retire earlier / volunteer your time
- Work at a job you love that pays less
- Buy some toys you have always wanted (motorcycle, boat, Jet Ski, etc.)
- Take a trip around the world
- Go back to school to get another degree
- And so much more . . . just put your mind to it and be creative!

Paying off your home early or having the money to pay off your home is in fact relatively simple to accomplish if you plan correctly. To accomplish this goal, you can use simple methods on your own or more complex methods that require the assistance of financial professionals. Some of these methods include:

- Biweekly mortgage payment plans
- Paying extra toward your mortgage every month
- Accelerator plans
- Equity separation

There are two schools of thought about paying off your mortgage. Some believe you should pay your mortgage off early, while others feel you should keep your mortgage forever and accumulate funds on the side to pay it off when you choose to do so. In my opinion, which method you should focus on will really depend on your retirement goals and your comfort level concerning money and finance. I will say that the belief system and the way things were done 25 to 50 years ago are much different today. Presently, a mortgage is viewed as more of a financial tool and as part of a wider scope of tools you have available to create wealth over time. Some view the mortgage as a debt like any other, a debt that they can't wait to get rid of; others regard the mortgage as an asset because of the tax benefits and financial liquidity it will provide to them.

Various methods in the marketplace can help you accelerate your wealth creation. There are other books worth reading on these subjects, which I will share with you at the end of this chapter.

These concepts are more than likely not going to be at the forefront of your mind when you are considering the purchase of your first home. As I previously stated, getting into your first home with the least amount of money down will be of primary concern. As the months roll by and as you feel more comfortable with your new home, you may begin to think about the long-term picture.

Before I explain each of the options, I want to show you in *Figure 12-4* how your principal and interest are split up based on a loan amortized over 30 years. You will note when you initially take out a mortgage that very little of your money will go toward principal. The bulk of your payment will go toward interest.

The point in *Figure 12-4* is to see that only a small percentage of your loan is being paid toward principal. *Figure 12-4* does not show this, but based on a 30-year amortization, it will be year 20 before your principal portion of your payment begins to exceed your interest payment. The idea behind paying your mortgage off early with biweekly payments or making

Principal & Interest Breakdown

$200,000 mortgage at 6.5% amortized over 30 years = $1,264.14 payment

	Paid to principal	Paid to interest
First payment	$180.80	$1,083.33
Second payment	$181.78	$1,082.35
Third payment	$182.77	$1,081.37
And so on…		

Figure 12-4

extra payments is to pay down the principal faster, thus reducing the amount of interest. Having said this, I will tell you about the various ways to pay off or save the money to pay off your mortgage early.

Biweekly Mortgage Payments

This concept has been around for a long time. The simple premise is that you pay half your mortgage payment every two weeks. The net result is that you end up making an extra payment in a year's period. You would knock six to eight years off of the length of time that you were anticipating to pay off your mortgage. Based on a $200,000 mortgage at 6.5% amortized over 30 years, you would pay off the mortgage in year 25, saving yourself roughly $60,658 in interest. To setup a biweekly plan, contact your lender as most lenders offer this service at no charge.

If you are an exceptionally disciplined individual and will be consistent, you can also just do this on your own by setting aside the money every two weeks and making the payment when your mortgage payment is due. To do this, take the amount of your mortgage payment, multiply it by 13, and then divide that figure by 12. You would then make that payment every month to your lender. In the example below, you would have an extra $104 per month going to your lender to pay down the principal balance of your mortgage loan:

$1,250 (monthly payment) × 13 = $16,250
$16,250 ÷ 12 = $1,354
Your new monthly payment would be $1,354
(or $677 every two weeks)

The bi-weekly mortgage plan is a simple plan that can be easily implemented. In the next section, I will show you a more calculated approach that can provide a more customized solution.

Paying Extra toward Your Mortgage Payment

Paying extra every month toward your mortgage is the simplest way to pay it off early. It's not a complex process to think about, and you can do it on your own. I also like this approach because you can calculate exactly when you want your mortgage paid off. So, if you want to have it paid off by age 42, you can calculate how much you need to pay every month to reach that goal. Let's look at some examples starting with *Figure 12-5*, which shows you the impact of making extra payments:

Impact of Making Extra Payments Toward Mortgage		
$200,000 loan at 6.5% amortized over 30 years		
Amount Extra	**Pay Off Time**	**Interest Savings**
$100 extra per month	24.30 years	$55,950
$200 extra per month	20.75 years	$90,019
$300 extra per month	18.17 years	$113,535
$400 extra per month	16.17 years	$130,813

Figure 12-5

You can see in *Figure 12-5* that making the extra payment every month will produce significant savings. If you were 26 years old and wanted to have your mortgage paid off by the age of 42, you would have to make $400 in extra payments every month to accomplish that goal.

Now, let's look at a more complex calculation of paying extra toward your mortgage in Figure *12-6*. We will use the same $200,000 loan at 6.5%

Impact of Extra Payments Using Portion of Rise			
	Monthly Extra		**Monthly Extra**
Year 1	$100	Year 7	$500
Year 2	$150	Year 8	$550
Year 3	$200	Year 9	$600
Year 4	$250	Year 10	$650
Year 5	$300	Year 11	$700
Year 6	$350	Year 12	$750
Year 7	$400	Year 13	$800
Year 8	$450	Year 14	$850
Pay off Date: 15.33 Years		**Interest Saved: $118,912**	

Figure 12-6

interest amortized over 30 years. However, considering the homeowner's income is going up every year, we will calculate an early pay off by contributing $50 of her $200 monthly raise toward the pay off amount on a yearly basis. In this example, the client will also be putting $100 more toward retirement and enjoying $50 of her raise for lifestyle / living purposes. Every year, she will continue to add $50 extra every month to the payoff of her mortgage.

Based on the 14-year plan of extra payments the client in *Figure 12-6* wanted, she would have her home paid off in 15.33 years. This scenario can be modified in any way, shape, or form depending on your own life/personal parameters. In the event of unexpected expenses, you could stop making the payments for a period and then resume them when your cash flow is back to normal. Assuming this client was 28 when she began this plan, she would be 43 when her mortgage is paid off. If she just made the regular payment every month for 30 years, she would be 58 years old when the mortgage is paid off.

Remember: the focus is to both contribute to savings/retirement and pay extra toward the mortgage. A prudent financial guiding principle is to spread your risk and reward around by not keeping all of your eggs in one basket. In this example, our homeowner added only $50 per month toward the mortgage while she added more to her investment savings and still had money left over to enjoy some of her favorite things.

There is so much flexibility to customize the pay off, depending on the borrower's needs. Like many other mortgage professionals, I use computer software to calculate these various pay off scenarios for clients. You can download a free trial version of the software I use by following a link to the author at www.whyownahome.com/info for 60 days. After the 60-day period, you will have to pay the author for the program.

Accelerator Plans

In a more complex approach to paying off your home early, there are a handful of lenders that offer what are known as "Accelerator Mortgage Plans." The idea behind these programs is to reduce the interest calculated on your mortgage balance using your monthly cash flow. These programs are offered by reputable mortgage lenders, and the mortgage professional you choose to work with can place you into this type of loan. This type of program is for someone who has already bought their first home, is now comfortable with homeownership, and is looking to explore ways to pay off the mortgage faster.

Instead of a 30-year fixed rate mortgage amortized over 30 years, your entire loan is a home equity loan/savings account combination. Your pay-check is put into your accelerator account as a direct deposit instead of your checking account. Since you have money sitting in your account between the time you receive it and the time you pay your bills, you are reducing the amount of interest that is being calculated on your loan. Since interest is calculated daily on home equity lines, the cash in your account in essence reduces your mortgage balance, thus reducing the interest you are being charged. Depending on how much cash you have sitting around on a monthly basis, you could have your home paid off in half the time or better using this type of loan product. The benefit to this program is that you are not changing your spending habits; you are just changing the place to where your direct deposit is going when you are paid. You pay all your bills as you normally would. The program, however, does assume you are putting money into savings on a monthly basis. If you are not saving monthly, then an accelerator program may not be effective for you.

Variations of this type of loan exist, but for the purposes of this chapter, I wanted to give you just a quick overview of how this loan program works. Lenders who offer these programs have simulators on their website so you can see how the program may work for you.

Visit www.whyownahome.com/info, to find links to lenders offering mortgage accelerator programs or talk with a mortgage professional to learn more.

Equity Separation

Equity separation is the most complex method to creating wealth; this is separate from paying your mortgage off. This method will require the use of a mortgage professional and a specialized financial planner. The power of this method is amazing, but it does require some education on your part. Furthermore, this method is designed mainly for someone who is buying their second or third home and who has created some net worth as a result of appreciation and investing/saving. It is also for someone who has a savings/investment plan and is disciplined in setting aside money every month. In the case of a first-time homebuyer, equity separation may make you think about putting less down than you planned so that you can maintain liquidity by having some cash on hand to deal with emergencies. As I have said before, you do not necessarily want to put all the money you have down on a home leaving your savings account down to an almost zero balance.

When using equity separation, you obtain an interest-only loan when you purchase a home, putting as little down as possible. You then take the extra money you would have contributed toward your down payment and place it into a side account where the money will be put into a safe and liquid investment using your financial advisor. Since you have an interest-only loan, you would then take the money you would have ordinarily paid to the lender for principal and place it into your side account, which will then be put into your safe and liquid investment once per year or at various times during the year.

Your investment could be in the form of a universal life insurance policy or some other type of investment that has minimal risk, but for which the rate of return would be equal to or better than the interest rate you would be paying on your mortgage.

In *Figure 12-7*, take a look at Hilda Homebuyer. She has worked hard and saved $30,000. She makes $75,000 per year putting her in the 31% tax bracket. She wants to buy a $150,000 condo. We will presume she has no additional money to save or pay down her mortgage for the next 30 years. Let's take a look at two scenarios. In the first scenario she puts the entire $30,000 down on a condo. In the second scenario, she puts only 5% ($7,500) down and invests the rest at a 6% average rate of return.

What lessons can you take away from the two scenarios in *Figure 12-7*?

1. Scenario 2 allowed Hilda to consistently have cash on hand. Had she lost her job or had a major unexpected expense, she would have still been able to pay her mortgage payment without the danger of potentially losing her home because of nonpayment.

2. In Scenario 1, she would have had no cash on hand since she put it all down on her home. Had she lost her job, she would have no money to continue making the mortgage payments and very well may have found herself in foreclosure. As a result, she would have not only lost her condo, but also the $30,000 she put down. As you have learned in this book, if she had put all of her money into her home and she had lost her job, it would not have been possible for her to get a new loan to take the money back out of the house without a job. In this case, she would have been stuck.

Equity Separation/Buying a Home/Comparing Interest Only

Scenario 1 (Big Down Payment)	Scenario 2 (Small Down Payment)
30-Year Fixed-Rate Mortgage 5.75% APR (interest rate) $30,000 Down Payment $0 left to invest	30-Year Interest-Only Mortgage 6.50% APR (interest rate) $7,500 Down Payment $22,500 left to invest
Payment & Taxes $700 Monthly Payment $592 After Tax Payment $625 After Tax Mortgage Payment	**Payment & Taxes** $813 Monthly Payment $93 For Mortgage Insurance 　(tax deductible)
Sends $100 extra to mortgage 　every month	Sends $100 to investments 　every month
After 7 Years (mortgage insurance falls off, home appreciated)	
Has No Savings Received $13,637 in tax savings	Has $44,615 in Savings and Investments Received $33,600 in tax savings
After 30 Years	
Received $28,587 in tax savings Has $85,980 in savings & investments	Received $100,801 in tax savings Added $93 per month to savings after year 7. Has $291,036 in savings & investments

*The assumption is that Hilda refinanced her mortgage after 15 years in Scenario 2 into another 15-year fixed-rate interest-only loan at the same rate. This example also assumes an annual average rate of return on investments of 6% (Per the Dow Jones, average rate of return for the S&P 500 is 10.47% from January 1, 1871 to December 31, 2008). The after-tax payment is calculated using the tax-deductible portion of the interest paid over the life of the loan and divided by the term to arrive at an average. With a fully amortized loan, the amount of interest paid annually is reduced, therefore reducing the tax savings. With an interest-only loan, the tax savings are always maximized since 100% of the monthly payment is tax-deductible. Furthermore, since she put less down, her loan amount was higher, resulting in greater tax savings. Please refer to Chapter 2 to learn more about how tax savings are calculated.

Figure 12-7

3. In Scenario 2, her monthly payment is only $33 more per month ($625 after tax payment less $592 after tax payment) than it is in Scenario 1.

4. After 30 years, in Scenario 2, Hilda accumulated assets in the amount of $291,036, which is $205,056 more than she would have had in Scenario 1. Once her home was paid off in Scenario 1, she began making the same payment into an investment account, which grew to $85,980 at the end of the 30 years. You can see that the delay in savings from the start in Scenario 1 meant a missed opportunity for her money to grow over time via compound interest.

5. If Hilda had chosen to, in Scenario 2, she could have paid off her mortgage balance of $142,500 and still have had $62,556 more than she would have had in Scenario 1. She is better off just continuing to make her monthly mortgage payment and continuing to take advantage of the tax savings our government provides.

6. She received $72,214 more in tax savings in Scenario 2 than in Scenario 1. (In this example, I have not calculated what she could have earned if she invested the majority of the tax savings that was provided to her in Scenario 2, which would have created even greater net worth).

7. In Scenario 2, she had peace of mind knowing she had money in the bank instead of living paycheck to paycheck.

8. In Scenario 2, Hilda had an interest-only loan. I purposely used a significantly higher interest rate that was .75% higher than Scenario 1 to illustrate that interest rate is not the only determining factor when considering mortgage money. In this example, this strategy Hilda had chosen would have not only

given her the flexibility of having cash on hand, but also allowed her to earn a greater return over time.

As you can see, with a little change in how Hilda managed her money and her mortgage, she created an additional $62,556 in cash over 30 years. The important point to take away from this is that you don't necessarily need to use all of your savings for a down payment. You can put some down and save the rest so you have cash available so you can handle emergencies if and when they arise and then get back on track with your savings goals. Remember, you want to create wealth, not a financial mess.

Those that follow the concepts of equity separation do it because they know the power of money and they want to be in control of their cash. As a first-time homebuyer, your concern may not necessarily be separating equity, but rather making sure you have enough cash set aside after a down payment. Using the bulk of the money you have for a down payment is not a prudent financial move as you leave yourself open to cash flow problems.

Although I currently have an interest-only loan on my home and strongly believe in them for the very purpose of separating equity, I am not promoting that you should have an interest-only loan. What I am promoting is that you take the time to learn about various loan programs and strategies that exist so you can make informed decisions about your situation. Keep in mind that loan programs that might best fit your needs may not even have an interest-only option available.

You should read up on these subjects and learn from licensed professionals who can pick up where I have left off regarding the discussion of equity separation and investing. I recommend the following books to learn more about equity separation and money management:

Missed Fortune 101 by Douglas Andrew
The New Rules of Money by Ric Edelman

These bestselling books will give you great insight into not only methods of separating your equity to create wealth, but also general investment knowledge so you can become educated and comfortable with the investing side of your life.

In concluding this chapter, I wanted to expose you to mortgage management strategies so that you have a complete understanding as to the decisions you make regarding your home and mortgage that impact your financial future. Although I do have my preferred strategies, my role as an advisor is to share with you the options that you have so you can then learn more and make informed decisions as to what strategy, if any, is best going to fit within your comfort zone. The last thing you want to happen as a consumer is to be talked into or "sold" a strategy or concept you are not comfortable with.

CONCLUSION

Going back to the analogy I opened this book with, you can see now that in order to reach your final destination on the flight of life, you must be prepared financially to do so. The financial benefits that go along with owning a home combined with your ability to save and invest will contribute to your comfortable flight. No doubt some turbulence will occur, but now you are prepared with the knowledge and tools to plan so that you have your ticket for the flight and you are able to manage any turbulence that comes along. When you get off the plane 30-40 years from now, you will step off with a smile and your favorite drink in hand and walk off to enjoy the next 30 years of retirement stress-free.

This book has hopefully served as both a "what not to do," as well as a "what to do" guide in attaining the goal of homeownership. The one hope that we all share is to one day become homeowners. And how responsible we are as homeowners will ultimately determine our financial futures.

My ultimate goal with this book was for you to begin to see how important your mortgage is and how vital it is to have a mortgage plan to guide you in creating wealth and security with your home. As you have read, owning a home doesn't have to be just about having property or paying down your mortgage, and it certainly shouldn't be about getting the biggest and the most expensive house on the block to keep up with the neighbors. If you are willing to get serious and be disciplined, you will have the opportunity to utilize homeownership, the right mortgage plan, and investments and savings to create financial stability. It doesn't have to be one or the other. If you plan properly, all these financial tools can work together to provide you with a solid financial future. So many factors are at play when you own a home, and it's up to you to decide which of those factors are most important and to design your mortgage plan so that it fits your financial life. Mortgage plans cannot be seen as one-size-fits-all; they can and must be tailored to your needs. And while you are mapping out which mortgage plan will fit your individual situation, you should also be very conscientious of both savings and retirement plans. They all go hand-in-hand.

The first step, however, is to delve into homeownership when the time is right for you. This will be the biggest financial undertaking of your life, and I truly hope you feel better informed, better educated, and more comfortable about "taking the plunge" as a result of reading this book. Once you have decided that owning a home is the right decision for you, the next step will be for you to do your research and find a reputable mortgage professional. The following step would be to sit down with him/her to discuss your interest in buying a home and how he/she can help you to make sure that purchasing a home is a suitable decision based on your own personal situation.

My hope for all of you who have taken the time to read this book is the same hope that I have for all of my clients (past, present, and future). That hope is to take the lessons learned from this book and create personal financial success through homeownership and proper financial planning.

TELL ME YOUR STORY

I would love to hear from you! Once you have purchased your new home, please feel free to send me a note along with some photos of you in front of your new home to let me know how this book helped you. As I mentioned previously, there is nothing more exciting for me than seeing the excitement on homebuyers' faces when they have purchased a home for the first time. So please take some time to share your joy with me.

Email your story and photos to: dboncosky@gmail.com

You can also email me to obtain my mailing address for sending pictures and letters via US Mail.

GLOSSARY

Definitions are a combination of my own along with official definitions from HUD.

Adjustable-Rate Mortgage (ARM)
>During the life of the loan the interest rate will change based on the index rate. Most adjustable-rate-mortgages have an initial fixed period.

After Repair Value (APV)
>The value of a home after it has been rehabilitated to fair market value. Term used when obtaining a FHA 203K loan.

Amortization
>A period of time the payments of a loan are spread out over. Example: 15 years, 30 years.

Annual Percentage Rate (APR)
>A measure of the cost of credit, expressed as a yearly rate after factoring in certain costs associated with the loan. It provides consumers with a good basis for comparing the cost of loans.

Application (1003 Loan Application)
>The first step in the official loan approval process; this universal form is used to record important information about the potential borrower necessary to the underwriting process.

Appraisal
>A document from a professional that gives an estimate of a property's fair market value based on the sales of comparable homes in the area and the features of a property; an appraisal is generally required by a lender before loan approval to ensure that

the mortgage loan amount is not more than the value of the property.

Appraised Value

An estimation of the current market value of a property.

Appreciation

An increase in property value.

Assets

Any item with measurable value.

Automated Underwriting

Loan processing completed through a computer-based system that evaluates past credit history to determine if a loan should be approved. This system removes the possibility of personal bias against the buyer.

Balloon Loan or Mortgage

A mortgage that typically offers low rates for an initial period of time (usually 5, 7, or 10) years; after that time period elapses, the balance is due or is refinanced by the borrower.

Bankruptcy

A federal law whereby a person's assets are turned over to a trustee and used to pay off outstanding debts; this usually occurs when someone owes more than they have the ability to repay.

Buy Down (Seller Buy Down)

Seller contributes money to buy down the interest rate for the seller.

Buyers Agent

A real estate agent who represents the buyer.

Closing
>The final step in property purchase where the title is transferred from the seller to the buyer. Closing occurs at a meeting between the buyer, seller, settlement agent, and other agents. At the closing the seller receives payment for the property. Also known as settlement.

Closing Costs
>Fees for final property transfer not included in the price of the property. Typical closing costs include charges for the mortgage loan such as origination fees, discount points, appraisal fee, survey, title insurance, legal fees, real estate professional fees, prepayment of taxes and insurance, and real estate transfer taxes.

Co-Signer (Co-borrower)
>A person that signs a credit application with another person, agreeing to be equally responsible for the repayment of the loan.

Comparative Market Analysis (COMPS)
>A property evaluation that determines property value by comparing similar properties sold within the last year.

Conforming loan
>Is a loan that does not exceed Fannie Mae's and Freddie Mac's loan limits. Freddie Mac and Fannie Mae loans are referred to as conforming loans.

Construction Loan
>A short-term, to finance the cost of building a new home. The lender pays the builder based on milestones accomplished during the building process. For example, once a sub-contractor pours the foundation and it is approved by inspectors the lender will pay for their service.

Contingency

A clause in a purchase contract outlining conditions that must be fulfilled before the contract is executed. Both, buyer or seller may include contingencies in a contract, but both parties must accept the contingency.

Conventional Loan

A loan that is not guaranteed or insured by the U.S. government (FHA or VA loan)

Counter Offer

A rejection to all or part of a purchase offer that negotiates different terms to reach an acceptable sales contract.

Credit Score

A numerical value determined by the three main credit reporting agencies, Experian, Equifax, and Trans Union. Scores range from about 350 - 850: a lower score meaning a person is a higher risk, while a higher score means that there is less risk.

Creditworthiness

The way a lender measures the ability of a person to qualify and repay a loan.

Debt-to-Income Ratio

A percentage of your income that can be allocated toward housing and overall expenses. Maximum conforming ratio is 28% of in come allowed for housing expense while 36% can be allocated for all expenses, including housing.

Deed

A document that legally transfers ownership of property from one person to another. The deed is recorded on public record with the property description and the owner's signature. Also known as the title.

Disclosures
> The release of relevant information about a property that may influence the final sale, especially if it represents defects or problems. "Full disclosure" usually refers to the responsibility of the seller to voluntarily provide all known information about the property.

Discount Point (Points)
> Prepayment to the lender to buy a lower interest rate. Normally 1% of the loan amount which provides the borrower with ¼% less in interest rate.

Down Payment
> The portion of a home's purchase price that is paid in cash and is not part of the mortgage loan.

Dual Agent
> A real estate agent who represents the buyer and the seller.

Earnest Money (Deposit)
> Money put down with the offer to purchase by a potential buyer to show good faith that they are serious about purchasing the home.

Equity
> An owner's financial interest in a property; calculated by subtracting the amount still owed on the mortgage loan(s) from the fair market value of the property. (property value – loan balance = equity).

Escrow Account
> A separate account into which the lender puts a portion of each monthly mortgage payment; an escrow account provides the funds needed for property taxes and homeowners insurance.

FSBO (For Sale by Owner)
>A home that is offered for sale by the owner without the use of a real estate agent.

Fair Market Value
>The price of a home that a buyer and a seller agree upon.

Fannie Mae: Federal National Mortgage Association (FNMA)
>A federally-chartered enterprise owned by private stockholders that purchases residential mortgages and converts them into securities for sale to investors; by purchasing mortgages, Fannie Mae supplies funds that lenders may loan to potential homebuyers.

FHA (Federal Housing Administration
>Established in 1934 to advance homeownership opportunities for all Americans; assists homebuyers by providing mortgage insurance to lenders to cover most losses that may occur when a borrower defaults; this encourages lenders to make loans to borrowers who might not qualify for conventional mortgages.

First Mortgage
>The mortgage with the first priority. In the event of default, the first mortgage holder will be paid first with any proceeds from the sale of the home.

Fixed-Rate Mortgage:
>A mortgage with payments that remain the same throughout the life of the loan.

Float
>Interest rate fluctuates with the market until locked.

Foreclosure
>A legal process where the lender takes back the home from a borrower who defaulted on the loan.

Freddie Mac: Federal Home Loan Mortgage Corporation (FHLM)
> A federally chartered corporation that purchases residential mortgages, securitizes them, and sells them to investors; this provides lenders with funds for new homebuyers.

Gift
> If someone gives you money for a down payment or gives the equity in a home you are buying.

Ginnie Mae: Government National Mortgage Association (GNMA)
> A government-owned corporation overseen by the U.S. Department of Housing and Urban Development, Ginnie Mae pools FHA-insured and VA-guaranteed loans to back securities for private investment.

Good Faith Estimate
> An estimate of all closing fees including pre-paid and escrow items as well as lender charges; must be given to the borrower within three days after submission of a loan application.

Gross Income
> Your earnings before taxes taken out.

Hazard Insurance (Homeowner's Insurance)
> An insurance policy, also called homeowner's insurance, that provides protection against damage to a dwelling and its contents including fire, storms or other damages. The policy also provides protection against claims of negligence or inappropriate action that result in someone's injury or property damage.

HO-6 / Content / Renters Insurance
> Insurance to protect your personal contents contained within a condominium, townhouse, or apartment.

Home
> A piece of residential real estate to which you hold the title.

Home Equity Line of Credit (Home Equity Loan)
> A mortgage loan, usually a second mortgage, allowing a borrower to obtain cash against the equity of a home, up to a predetermined amount.

Home Inspection
> An examination of the structure and mechanical systems to determine a home's quality, soundness and safety; makes the potential homebuyer aware of any repairs that may be needed. The homebuyer generally pays inspection fees.

Home Warranty
> Offers protection for mechanical systems and attached appliances against unexpected repairs not covered by homeowner's insurance; coverage extends over a specific time period and does not cover the home's structure.

Homeowner's Insurance
> An insurance policy, also called hazard insurance, that provides protection against damage to a dwelling and its contents including fire, storms or other damages. The policy also provides protection against claims of negligence or inappropriate action that result in someone's injury or property damage.

HUD
> The U.S. Department of Housing and Urban Development; established in 1965, HUD works to create a decent home and suitable living environment for all Americans; it does this by addressing housing needs, improving and developing American communities, and enforcing fair housing laws.

HUD1 Statement

Also known as the "settlement statement," or "closing statement" it itemizes all closing costs related to the loan. It shows how much money is either required by or given to the parties involved in the transaction.

Inquiry

Each time a copy of your credit report is viewed by a lender is known as an inquiry.

Installment Debt

Is debt that must be repaid in a specific period of time. Example: car loan or mortgage.

Interest

A fee charged for the use of borrowing money.

Interest Only

A loan which only pay interest on the money borrowed.

Interest Rate

The amount of interest charged on a monthly loan payment, ex pressed as a percentage.

Judgment

A legal decision; when requiring debt repayment, a judgment may include a property lien that secures the creditor's claim by providing a collateral source.

Jumbo Loan

Is a loan that exceeds Fannie Mae's and Freddie Mac's loan limits. Freddie Mac and Fannie Mae loans are referred to as conforming loans.

Liabilities

A person's financial obligations such as long-term / short-term debt.

Lien

A legal claim against property that must be satisfied when the property is sold. A claim of money against a property, wherein the value of the property is used as security in repayment of a debt.

Liquid Asset (Liquidity)

A cash asset or an asset that is easily converted into cash.

Listing Agent

A real estate agent who represents the seller of a home

Listing Agreement

A contract between a seller and a real estate agent to market and sell a home. A listing agreement obligates the real estate agent to seek qualified buyers, report all purchase offers and help negotiate the highest possible price and most favorable terms for the property seller.

Loan Fraud

Purposely giving incorrect information on a loan application in order to better qualify for a loan; may result in civil liability or criminal penalties.

Loan to Value (LTV) Ratio

A percentage calculated by dividing the amount borrowed by the price or appraised value of the home to be purchased ($140,000 loan amount / $180,000 value = 78% LTV).

Lock-In

>   Since interest rates can change frequently, many lenders offer an
>   interest rate lock-in that guarantees a specific interest rate if the
>   loan is closed within a specific time.

Mortgage

>   A lien on the property that secures the promise to repay a loan. The
>   mortgage gives the lender the right to collect payment on the loan
>   and to foreclose if the loan obligations are not met.

Mortgage Insurance

>   A policy that protects lenders against some or most of the losses
>   that can occur when a borrower defaults on a mortgage loan;
>   mortgage insurance is required primarily for borrowers with a
>   down payment of less than 20% of the home's purchase price.

Mortgage Insurance Premium (MIP)

>   A monthly payment -usually part of the mortgage payment - paid
>   by a borrower for mortgage insurance when less than 20% has been
>   put down for a conventional loan.

Mortgagee

>   The lender in a mortgage agreement.

Mortgagor

>   The borrower in a mortgage agreement

Negative Amortization

>   Negative amortization occurs when the monthly payments do not
>   cover all of the interest cost. The interest cost that isn't covered is
>   added to the unpaid principal balance.

Non-Conforming loan
> Is a loan that exceeds Fannie Mae's and Freddie Mac's loan limits. Freddie Mac and Fannie Mae loans are referred to as conforming loans.

Non-Preferred Debt
> Is non-tax-deductible debt such as credit card debt or car loan.

PITI
> Principal, Interest, Taxes, and Insurance: the four elements of a monthly mortgage payment; payments of principal and interest go directly towards repaying the loan while the portion that covers taxes and insurance (homeowner's and mortgage, if applicable) goes into an escrow account to be paid when they are due.

PMI: Private Mortgage Insurance
> A monthly payment -usually part of the mortgage payment - paid by a borrower for mortgage insurance when less than 20% has been put down for a conforming loan.

Points
> Prepayment to the lender to buy a lower interest rate. Normally 1% of the loan amount which provides the borrower with ¼% less in interest rate.

Pre-Approval
> A lender commits to lend to a potential borrower a fixed loan amount based on a completed loan application, credit reports, debt, savings and has been reviewed by an underwriter or an automated underwriting system.

Preferred Debt
> Is tax-deductible debt such as mortgage interest, real estate taxes, and in some cases, mortgage insurance.

Prepaid expenses
> Is the daily interest on the loan from the day you close until the end of that month. In some cases, the prepayment of your escrow money may be considered a prepaid expense.

Prepayment
> Any amount paid to reduce the principal balance of a loan before the due date or payment in full of a mortgage prior to the full amortization.

Prepayment Penalty
> A provision in some loans that charge a fee to a borrower who pays off a loan before it is due.

Pre-Qualify
> A lender informally determines the maximum amount an individual is eligible to borrow. This is not a guaranty of a loan.

Prime Rate
> The base interest rate that is offered by banks for home equity lines. Depending on the lender and the borrower's circumstances, the prime rate may be marked up or down.

Principal
> The amount of money borrowed to buy a home or the amount of the loan that has not been paid back to the lender.

Qualifying Ratios (debt-to-income ratios)
> A percentage of your income that can be allocated toward housing and overall expenses. Maximum conforming ratio is 28% of income allowed for housing expense while 36% can be allocated for all expenses, including housing.

Radon

> A radioactive gas found in some homes that, if occurring in strong enough concentrations, can cause health problems.

Rate Cap

> A limit on an ARM on how much the interest rate or mortgage payment may change. Rate caps limit how much the interest rates can rise or fall on the adjustment dates and over the life of the loan.

Rate Lock

> A commitment by a lender to a borrower guaranteeing a specific interest rate over a period of time at a set cost.

Revolving Debt

> Includes accounts in which the balance changes each month with the minimum monthly payment. There is no end date for the debt. Example: credit card debt.

Rider

> An add on to an insurance policy for additional coverage.

Risk Based Pricing

> Fee structure used by creditors based on risks of granting credit to a borrower with a poor credit history.

Second Mortgage

> An additional mortgage on property. In case of a default the first mortgage must be paid before the second mortgage. Second mortgages are more risky for the lender and usually carry a higher interest rate.

Term Life Insurance

> Is insurance to provide a predetermined amount of money upon death to a beneficiary. Basic form of life insurance.

Title
> A legal document establishing the right of ownership and is recorded to make it part of the public record. Also known as a Deed.

Title Insurance
> Insurance that protects the lender against any claims that arise from arguments about ownership of the property. An insurance policy guaranteeing the accuracy of a title search protecting against errors.

Trade Lines
> Lines of credit you have that are reflected on your credit report. Example: credit cards.

Transfer Taxes
> State and local taxes charged for the transfer of real estate. Usually equal to a percentage of the sales price.

Truth-in-Lending
> A federal law obligating a lender to give full written disclosure of all fees, terms, and conditions associated with the loan initial period and then adjusts to another rate that lasts for the term of the loan. Known as the disclosure of the Annual Percentage Rate.

Underwriting
> The process of analyzing a loan application to determine the amount of risk involved in making the loan; it includes a review of the potential borrower's credit history and a judgment of the property value.

VA Loans (Department of Veterans Affairs)
> A federal agency, which guarantees loans made to veterans; similar to mortgage insurance, a loan guarantee protects lenders against loss that may result from a borrower default.

Whole Life Insurance

> Is an insurance policy to provide money upon death to a beneficiary. This type of policy has an investment component to it which can grow in value over time. Universal, variable, and traditional are the three options.

INDEX

ABOUT THE AUTHOR

Douglas Boncosky helps people with financing and managing their mortgage debt and equity structure to create wealth. Doug's comprehensive approach to preparing clients for life as a homeowner was the motivation behind writing Create Wealth With Homeownership. Doug is currently a practicing mortgage professional in the Chicago suburbs. He is a member of the Illinois Association of Mortgage Professionals, National Association of Mortgage Brokers, and is Licensed by the State of Illinois Department of Financial and Professional Regulation – Division of Banking. Doug speaks on the subject matter of homebuying and home finance to members and employees of corporations, organizations, and private groups.

Douglas Boncosky
dboncosky@gmail.com

www.dougboncosky.com
My website for my mortgage practice.

www.whyownahome.com
My website for this book.